How 

Introducing this season's hottest
Harlequin Medical Romance novels packed with
your summertime dose of dreamy doctors,
pulse-racing drama and sizzling romantic tension!
Fly up, up and away and follow these
globe-trotting docs as they travel to stunning
international destinations for work...but end up
finding a special someone in their arms!

Grab your passport and find out in

Second Chance in Santiago by Tina Beckett
One Night to Sydney Wedding by JC Harroway
The Doctor's Italian Escape by Annie Claydon
Spanish Doc to Heal Her by Karin Baine
ER Doc's South Pole Reunion by Juliette Hyland
Their Accidental Vegas Vows by Amy Ruttan

All available now!

Dear Reader,

When I got asked to write a Jet Set romance, I needed to set it in the South Pole. I'm fascinated by the stations there. Plus, it is the absolute *best* place to force characters together because they cannot escape. I knew from page one I was going to enjoy giving Sam and Forrest the happily-ever-after they deserve.

Dr. Sam Miller has fallen in love twice. Both times his heart has gotten smashed. First by his best friend turned lover, Forrest, who walked away without a reason. Then by his fiancé, who found comfort with another. Now he's determined not to set down roots. It's going exactly to plan, until Forrest shows up. It's too easy to fall into old habits. Too easy to fall—again—for the man he's never forgotten.

Dr. Forrest Wilson's family made sure he knew he was never enough. He completed med school but crashed and burned at bedside, then turned to the lab. He fell in love, once, but walked away so his lover had a chance at finding better. So why is Sam at the South Pole? Alone? And is it possible their South Pole reunion could turn into forever?

Juliette Hyland

ER DOC'S SOUTH POLE REUNION

JULIETTE HYLAND

MEDICAL ROMANCE

If you purchased this book without a cover you should be aware that this book is stolen property. It was reported as "unsold and destroyed" to the publisher, and neither the author nor the publisher has received any payment for this "stripped book."

**Harlequin®
MEDICAL
ROMANCE**

ISBN-13: 978-1-335-94312-5

ER Doc's South Pole Reunion

Copyright © 2025 by Juliette Hyland

All rights reserved. No part of this book may be used or reproduced in any manner whatsoever without written permission.

Without limiting the author's and publisher's exclusive rights, any unauthorized use of this publication to train generative artificial intelligence (AI) technologies is expressly prohibited.

This is a work of fiction. Names, characters, places and incidents are either the product of the author's imagination or are used fictitiously. Any resemblance to actual persons, living or dead, businesses, companies, events or locales is entirely coincidental.

For questions and comments about the quality of this book, please contact us at CustomerService@Harlequin.com.

TM and ® are trademarks of Harlequin Enterprises ULC.

 Harlequin Enterprises ULC
22 Adelaide St. West, 41st Floor
Toronto, Ontario M5H 4E3, Canada
www.Harlequin.com

Printed in U.S.A.

Juliette Hyland began crafting heroes and heroines in high school. She lives in Ohio with her Prince Charming, who has patiently listened to many rants regarding characters failing to follow the outline. When not working on fun and flirty happily-ever-afters, Juliette can be found spending time with her beautiful daughters, giant dogs or sewing uneven stitches with her sewing machine.

Books by Juliette Hyland

Harlequin Medical Romance

Alaska Emergency Docs

One-Night Baby with Her Best Friend

Boston Christmas Miracles

A Puppy on the 34th Ward

Hope Hospital Surgeons

Dating His Irresistible Rival
Her Secret Baby Confession

Fake Dating the Vet

Harlequin Romance

Falling for His Fake Date

If the Fairy Tale Fits...

Beauty and the Brooding CEO

Royals in the Headlines

How to Win a Prince
How to Tame a King

Visit the Author Profile page
at Harlequin.com for more titles.

For reformed perfectionists and those still finding their way. You are enough, just the way you are.

**Praise for
Juliette Hyland**

"A delightful second chance on love with intriguing characters, powerful back stories and tantalizing chemistry! Juliette Hyland quickly catches her reader's attention.... I really enjoyed their story! I highly recommend this book.... The story line has a medical setting with a whole lot of feels in the mix!"
—*Goodreads* on *Falling Again for the Single Dad*

PROLOGUE

The ship wasn't going to sink. It wasn't going to sink. It wasn't.

The mental ramblings sloshed against Dr. Sam Miller's brain as he made his way toward the on-board clinic. The Drake Passage was a notoriously difficult stretch of sea. He'd known that when he'd signed up to work at the McMurdo Station at the South Pole.

Hell, his mother had sent him every social media video she could find about the trip. Her algorithm must have been hyperfocused on the Drake Passage, given the volume of related content that had landed in his text messages.

It had been sweet, and he'd reassured her each time that he knew what he was doing. He'd worked in remote locations for the last five years as a traveling doctor assigned to emergency clinics in the wilderness. He *hadn't* told her about the time he'd been on a prop plane headed to a remote Alaskan village, and he'd been certain he was going to die in a fiery crash.

That hadn't happened.

And this ship wasn't sinking, either.

Didn't mean his brain wasn't pushing doubts through his nervous system. But he'd ignored the heightened awareness for years. His parents claimed he was an adrenaline junkie, constantly seeking out locations with at least some sense of danger. He disagreed, but he knew one of the most important jobs a parent had was to keep their child safe.

So he'd answered every worried text. And had no intention of letting his mother know exactly how unsteady the trip through the passage really was.

"Doctor Miller, so glad to see you." Dr. Nicole Sapson gripped the edge of the table like a pro as the ship rolled again.

Sam didn't have the same dexterity and, before he knew what was happening, he was pressed up against the wall.

"Still getting your sea legs, I see." She let out a low chuckle.

"How does anyone get used to this?" He braced himself against the wall and took a deep breath.

"It's the Drake Passage." She rolled her head from one side to the other. Apparently, no other answer was needed. "I've seen most of the ship's residents today. All needing medication for sea sickness. I appreciate you stepping in for me while my nurse practitioner is under the weather."

"Of course." After working in remote locations, Sam understood the need for relief. He'd worked in two locations where he was the only physician for a hundred miles. He'd delivered babies, provided trauma care and stitched up little ones from falls. All while chronically exhausted. So he was more than willing to provide support when others needed it.

"Like I said, I've seen most everyone headed for McMurdo, it seems like. Ordered them to stay in their rooms while we finish riding out the rolling.

They will be most comfortable there." As soon as the words were out of her mouth, the ship rolled again.

Luckily, this time Sam was more prepared. Barely.

"If you need me—" Dr Sapson started. Her worried gaze was focused on his less than steady legs.

"I will be fine, Doctor Sapson. Get rest—now. I won't be on the boat headed back."

"But the doctors you are replacing at McMurdo will be." She winked as she headed for the door.

"Touché."

Sam looked around the little clinic. He'd helped out once before and knew his way about, but the ship hadn't been tilting in all directions then. So he headed to the small closet where the meds and supplies were located. Always a good idea to start by making sure he was well acquainted with what he had to work with.

"Anyone here? Please?"

The low call sent a buzz through Sam's already overloaded nervous system.

It wasn't Forrest Wilson on the other side of the supply door. Couldn't be.

His former best friend, turned lover, had ended things years ago, just as Sam had been headed for residency in emergency medicine in New York. Ended things and taken a residency in internal medicine in Seattle, as far across the country as he could get.

I love you, but you deserve more.

The words were seared into Sam's heart. Nothing he had said in response had mattered. The man had disappeared from his life after years of being Sam's anchor. Left him reeling.

Forrest was not here now. He wasn't.

"Anyone? I have a migraine." There was a long sigh at the end of the word of *migraine*.

Forrest had suffered from migraines. Just a coincidence. Sam grabbed the medication he needed, no matter who was on the other side of the door, and headed out into the clinic to meet his patient.

"Sam?" Forrest pinched his eyes closed and reopened them.

"Not a migraine hallucination, Forrest." Sam forced the words out despite his tongue's near refusal to move. Forrest was here. On the ship to McMurdo. Outside of the crew, everyone would be getting off and heading to the station for the winter.

For eight months.

The man looked good. Even breathing through his teeth and holding his hand over his eyes to cap the light. His dark hair was mussed. The three-day-old growth on his chin showed how bad he felt.

Forrest always kept his face free of hair. Something his grandmother had drilled into him as a young man.

There was a woman Sam had not mourned. He'd attended the ceremony to support Forrest only. She'd made the man he loved feel worthless no matter what he achieved. If there was an afterlife, Sam hoped she was answering for every bitter tirade she'd leveled at Forrest.

Sam moved and dimmed the lights. "Better? Or do you need them all the way off?"

"Better." Forrest rubbed his chin and Sam turned them all the way off.

"You still rub your chin when you're lying."

They'd roomed together in college, a random piece of luck of the draw that had worked out better than either could have expected. Been best friends until med school when one night, a silly game of spin the bottle with their group of overtired friends had finally lit the fuse of something Sam had wanted for so long.

Their love had burned bright and Sam had started to think about weddings and forever. Until Forrest had just walked away, two days before Sam had planned to ask him to marry him.

For nearly their entire twenties he'd lived with this man, loved him. And apparently, he still knew his tells.

"I didn't know you were working as a ship's doctor. I thought emergency medicine was the aim." Forrest took the small plastic cup of migraine pills Sam passed him.

Did he make sure our fingers didn't touch? And why am I noticing?

Sam bit the inside of his cheek hoping that would stop the racing thoughts.

"I'm not. I'm just helping Dr. Sapson while her NP is under the weather. She needed a break and I figured since I am not seasick…" He shrugged as the ramblings echoed in the quiet.

"I'm headed to McMurdo. I'm the primary facility doctor for the winter rotation."

Forrest blinked and looked like he was at a loss for words. Sam didn't blame him for needing a minute to adjust to the idea of eight months being co-located with Sam, not to cope with the migraine ripping through his head.

Then he nodded and crossed his arms. "I work for a research company—I'm working on a project studying human immune responses in isolated conditions. I'll be in the McMurdo lab every day trying to see…well, lots of things. Probably won't be out of the lab much."

"Lab?" That didn't make sense. Forrest hadn't been headed for research. Sure, he hadn't liked the fast pace of the ER or surgery, but that hadn't been an issue because he had planned, had *wanted* to branch into internal medicine. The pace was slower there, mostly because they were constantly waiting on lab results.

"Yeah. It's a government research grant. Immune response in isolated conditions." He pinched his eyes closed. "I already said that. Migraine makes it hard to think. I'm the internal medicine doc guiding the study. So I will be in the lab constantly."

Don't expect to see me.

Message received loud and clear.

He'd known doctors that took a year's sabbatical to get away from patients. Sam couldn't imagine that of Forrest, but if he had needed a break, then retreating to the lab made sense for an internal medicine specialist.

Not that Sam planned to ask.

The ship rolled and Sam caught the back of the counter just like Nicole. Forrest didn't have the same luck.

He knocked into Sam, his scent racing through Sam's body. One arm wrapped around Forrest's waist, catching at least some of the blow against Forrest's hips.

"Oof." Forrest moved as soon as the ship was steady. "Thanks for the catch. I should get going. Um." He looked around and was out the door before any other words could be said.

Eight months. They had eight months in one of the most desolate places on earth.

And he told me not to expect to see him.

Maybe that was for the best. Forrest had closed that door almost eight years ago. No sense reopening a scar Sam had worked so hard to heal.

CHAPTER ONE

THE LAST FLIGHT into McMurdo for the winter season had nearly finished unloading the final supplies it was dropping off. And when it left, so did every excuse Dr. Forrest Wilson had for avoiding Sam. The first three weeks he'd managed. Barely.

The urge to stop by the clinic, to knock on his quarters, had pushed against his chest from the moment he'd seen Sam on the ship. Sam Wilson.

Best friend. Boyfriend. The one he'd let go.

There were many tags Forrest could assign to the man. Sam wasn't supposed to be here. The man wanted marriage, a settled life. Not months in the wilderness.

Why is he here?

That was something he was probably going to find out now that Dr. Anderson, the other physician assigned to the McMurdo clinic, was headed back to the States for cancer treatment. He'd be on that final flight when it left. Forrest wasn't sure what the first indicators were, but a routine blood test a week ago had uncovered the markers for blood cancer.

One that must be fast-moving since everyone on station had been required to have a full medical workup before arriving. If the markers had been there when those tests were done, no one would have cleared Dr. Anderson for eight months at McMurdo.

There wasn't time to get another doctor here. When the flight left today, Forrest would become

Sam's official backup. But there were two nurse practitioners working in the clinic full-time—so his and Sam's interactions would be limited.

Sure. Lying to myself is always a good idea.

Forrest closed his eyes in what he knew would be a failed attempt to ignore his inner voice. His grandmother had complained constantly that he was too lost in his head. That he was lazy, no matter how many chores he completed. He was never enough for her, no matter how much he seemed to work.

"Why don't you stop by the clinic today? I can walk you through what's there." Sam's voice was barely audible above the wind on the loading dock. He was standing less than a foot from him. Closer than he'd been in years.

If I don't count the ship's clinic.

Forrest had made sure he hadn't touched Sam when he'd passed him the pills for his migraine. He'd monitored his fingers to ensure no accidental brush.

Getting over Sam had been the hardest thing he had ever done.

He'd wanted the best for Sam. And the best wasn't Forrest. He'd grown up knowing that. And residency had reinforced it. Sam was nearly perfect and Forrest... Forrest was very much not. He wasn't strong enough to walk back through that door.

"Do you think you will need me often? I have my research." Research that was not all-consuming. Yes, there were labs to run. But tests took time to complete their cycles. Only then could he analyze the results.

He'd hidden in the lab so much that the other partner on the study, Dr. Charlee Lons, constantly gave him a hard time.

She insisted they were allowed free time. That it was even encouraged, as studies showed the human brain operated better when it had regular creative breaks.

There is a reason we call it STEAM now, instead of just STEM. You need the arts.

The proof that Charlee truly lived by her favorite line hung in frames near the door of the lab—beautiful watercolors she'd done herself. She'd already done four in the time they'd been there, one a week.

Everyone was encouraged to bring something fun to the station. Something to occupy the time. Forrest had brought a guitar and picked out a song or two when he was in his room. But he'd learned to play with Sam. *That* guitar was at home. A prize he'd never risk. And every time he picked up the substitute instrument he'd brought, happy memories rotated through his mind. It only made the urge to seek out Sam grow, so he'd put the guitar away.

He pushed himself in the gym, but his mind still found it far too easy to walk the paths back to Sam.

Why is he here?

Sam was meant to be in New York. Meant to be happy and settled—with the perfect partner he'd always wanted. The life he'd had all planned out. He'd always wanted the perfect life his parents had. Soulmates, Sam called them.

Forrest no longer believed he'd never marry anyone. Or rather, after therapy, he wasn't afraid of the idea of commitment anymore. But he also wasn't looking for a soulmate. He had no reason to believe they existed, at least not for him. His own family was far from perfect, and they'd reminded him every chance they got that he was a mistake.

He was barely looking for a partner. He'd been on three dates in the last five years. All of them busts. Now he huddled in the lab: at least specimen slides never judged you.

"Earth to Forrest." Sam's fingers snapped in his line of sight. "Did you hear any of that?"

"No." Forrest shook his head, like that could force the attention he sometimes had trouble finding to the forefront. "Sorry, Sam. I wasn't expecting this and I haven't worked with patients in years outside of a lab setting."

On paper he was an internist, a doctor of internal medicine, but he was also an immunologist who kept to the labs these days. Patients in studies were screened. In fact, most of the time, Forrest only had to work with blind data.

No telling anyone bad news. No bacterial infection overwhelming antibiotics. No family to deliver the ultimate devastation to, then returning to the grind like nothing had happened.

"The good news is I work with patients every day. And this is my fifth remote location in five years. In fact, at the last place I was the only attending. I pretty much slept at that hospital." Sam rolled his head, loosening his shoulder muscles.

He's tired.

Time and distance hadn't stopped Sam from knowing when Forrest was lying back in the ship's clinic. And it wasn't stopping Forrest from seeing the exhaustion coating Sam. The man was a perfectionist. And he nearly always achieved his goals. That didn't mean he could do everything himself. Sam needed help.

And now Forrest was looking for ways to dodge the extra assignment.

This was why he'd let Sam go. Why he'd made sure Sam knew he was too good for Forrest. That he deserved more.

"I assumed you'd be working in New York City. Working your way up to head of the emergency department in record time. That was your goal. The ten-year plan you talked about before heading off to residency. Why are you moving so much?"

The question struck a sore spot.

Someone who hadn't lived with Sam for most of his twenties might miss the subtle shift of his gray-blue eyes. Forrest wasn't sure why, but the question had hurt.

"Forget I asked." Forrest started to reach out, but Sam stepped back. Forrest swallowed the pain as he tried to cover the embarrassment by crossing his arms.

"Life's paths are weird." Sam shrugged as the plane carrying Dr. Anderson took off. "I wouldn't have expected to find you in the South Pole, either."

"No. I was more a North Pole guy." The joke flew

from Forrest's mouth. Sam had affectionately complained every November that Christmas decor wasn't supposed to go up until after Thanksgiving.

It was the fight they had most often and, given that Sam helped him decorate for six Novembers in a row, one could hardly call it a fight. Forrest still had each of the clay Christmas ornaments they'd bought at the mall stall when they were together. Little men in snow hats with their names underneath. Snowmen holding hands. A new clay scene each year.

His grandmother had hated anything to do with the season. Hated those stalls with the cheesy ornaments. Forrest didn't put them on his tree anymore, but they were lovingly wrapped in bubble wrap at the bottom of his ornament bin. Precious, hidden cargo.

"I am pretty sure Santa isn't there. And definitely sure that he'd agree Christmas decor shouldn't be up until December first." Sam cleared his throat as he looked around the loading bay.

The now largely empty loading bay.

This was the way they'd been for so long. Easy conversations. Jokes. Serious talks that lasted for hours without either noticing the passage of time. It had been easy then to believe Forrest could fit in Sam's life. But unlike Sam, for him something had always felt off in med school. He had been good at it, but the passion Sam had clearly felt had just never materialized.

He was a puzzle piece that didn't fit in Sam's perfect picture no matter how hard he tried to jam himself into position.

That had been true eight years ago when they were in their late twenties. It was true today at thirty-six. Which meant sliding back into old patterns would be a mistake.

Still, he couldn't stop the words rising in his throat, clamoring to answer Sam's jest. "I think the South Pole probably has a direct line to the North Pole. Maybe while I am here, I can contact the station up there and have them radio the old man. Settle this argument once and for all." He raised his chin waiting for the next playful dig.

But Sam waved the comment away. "It hardly matters now. We can both decorate whenever we want." He turned to go. "Please stop by the clinic as soon as you get a chance. If I am out of the clinic, I want to make sure you know where everything is and are up to speed. Patients are the most important thing."

Then he was gone. The wind bit through the thermal jacket and Forrest knew he needed to head in, too. But he couldn't force his feet to move.

Sam had stopped the banter. And reminded him that the argument hardly mattered anymore.

He was right. But that didn't fix the hole ripping open through Forrest's soul.

Sam ran his hand through his hair as he stepped into the quiet clinic. With any luck, he'd skirted the worst-case scenario for Dr. Anderson. The man was on the plane and already scheduled with an oncologist.

Running the blood test on the physician had been a stroke of luck. One that might have saved the man's life. His cancer was moving fast, and being trapped in the Antarctic was the worst-case scenario.

I should be happy. I should celebrate the success.

This was about as perfect as possible. Less than a week from initial complaint to the call to Houston requesting Dr. Anderson get on the last flight out when the final supply run came in. Sam prided himself on running as close to perfect in every setting. He should be happy.

He'd done the complete blood count, commonly called a CBC, to rule out mono and iron deficiencies when the doctor's exhaustion had continued despite several days of ordered rest. The white cell count was off the charts and his red blood cells dangerously low. It was a shocking differential from the tests they'd all had run before agreeing to this gig. A bad sign.

He'd ordered the evac before even waking Dr. Anderson from yet another much-needed nap. The head of the Center for Polar Medical Operations, based in Texas, had agreed with Sam's assessment and pointed out there was no one they could send to replace Anderson.

And Sam had mentioned Forrest. A mistake he'd regretted every moment since. Yes, the Center for Polar Medical Operations would have identified him. After all, he was on the reserve list. Everyone at the station with additional skills understood they might be called to use them when needed. It was in their contract for the pole that their mission could change if necessary.

His boss thought it was great that he already knew Forrest and had asked him to get in touch. Sam had lied; said he didn't know Dr. Wilson. Said he only checked the list because he recognized a replacement was needed.

It was sort of the truth. Sort of. He didn't know *this* Forrest. He knew the man he'd lived with for years. Or maybe he hadn't known him either, since Forrest had walked away with such ease.

Sam had believed they were soulmates. Meant for each other. And then Forrest had simply left. No fanfare. No discussion. Just that one sentence and he'd vanished from their shared life.

I love you, but you deserve more.

And now Sam was going to have to work with him again.

Luckily, his boss had agreed to get in touch with the group in charge of Forrest's research and let them know he'd need to sub in from time to time.

He'd promised to let Sam know if there were any issues. None had arisen. Forrest had agreed to the arrangement, or maybe he'd been told there was no other choice. That instead of spending all his time in the lab he'd have to serve in the hospital, too. With Sam.

But Dr. Anderson was safe. That was what mattered.

I am a selfish ass.

Because instead of celebrating the success, Sam was moping. All because Forrest had been forced to work in the clinic on rotation.

He'd looked for the man every chance he was out of the clinic. Every meal. Every social function—not that Sam had stayed at any of them. Or talked to many people. But he noticed all of them had the same thing in common. Forrest's absence.

Today when Forrest had pointed out the need to be in his lab, Sam had nearly snapped that the doctor he'd known had loved clinical work. Thrived at the bedside.

But that Forrest was gone. He'd chased a different dream. A dream he hadn't wanted to share with Sam eight years ago.

"Damn." Sam clenched his fists. He'd cried over his fiancé—*ex*-fiancé, Oliver's betrayal five years ago. Screamed at the universe's ability to gift him two loves and let him lose both. But the mourning he'd done over his failed engagement had been nothing like the dark period he'd dwelled in after Forrest left his life.

Maybe it had been made easier by finding Oliver in bed with another man.

His parents had the perfect marriage. Fifty-two years and counting. The pair of academics were tied at the hip, even working projects together. When anyone asked if they ever got sick of each other, they'd laugh and say *not yet*.

Sam craved that love. The idea of working with someone and loving them so much, it never got old. He yearned for the perfect person. The one who completed him.

Or he had, once upon a time. Not anymore. Now

he was a confirmed bachelor. Planning one failed proposal and then losing a few thousand dollars on wedding deposits was clearly the universe's way of saying *No soulmate for you*. He was fine with it.

It was easier to believe that when the object of that failed proposal wasn't trapped in the same place with him for the next seven months.

"Sam?" Forrest's voice was even, no hint that this was bothering him like it was Sam. "This a good time?"

He was the one that walked away. Of course he's fine.

Sam took a deep breath before looking up from the tablet that he'd been paying exactly zero attention to in the last few minutes. "I told you to stop by."

"Ordered it, really." Forrest held up his hand. "That sounded bad and is not what I meant at all. You pointed out the necessity for me to get to know the place for when I'm needed here. A more than fair request."

"Always the diplomat." The man avoided conflict like the plague. Sam hadn't dictated his attendance, but he'd not been welcoming, either. "I wasn't exactly friendly on the tarmac."

"You were seeing off a colleague with a fast-moving cancer. I think you're allowed to have feelings about that." Forrest took a deep breath, damn near mimicking the motion Sam had made when he'd walked into the clinic. "Let's start over. As colleagues. If we hadn't spent our twenties together, we'd be acting completely normal. What if we come at this as if there is no history between us? A get-to-know-the-clinic-and-colleagues session." Forrest smiled.

Is it that easy for him?

"Fine." It wasn't that simple for Sam, but he'd handle whatever emotions this brought privately. "I'm Sam. An emergency and trauma doctor. Over the last five years, I've worked in the Arctic Circle in Alaska, rural Wisconsin and Alabama, as well as mass trauma centers in New York City and Los Angeles."

"Damn." Forrest grinned. "That is impressive. I've been hiding in an Illinois research center for the last five years. No remote locations—unless you count the lab that I probably spend too much time in."

"Hiding in the lab? But you were great at bedside." That broke the rule. They were supposed to be starting fresh.

"Why aren't you climbing the rungs at a trauma center in a fast-moving city? That was your dream. One you'd talked about nearly every night. Why are you at the South Pole?"

He'd avoided the question by pointing out that Sam wasn't exactly chasing the dream he'd wanted, either.

He'd nearly had that dream. The hospital staff he'd worked with during the two years he'd dated Oliver had all joked they'd call him chief one day. More than one had tried to talk him out of turning in his notice.

Well, Sam could avoid questions, too.

"Most of the staff here have no chronic issues. Not surprising, given the medical tests required to winter over. So hopefully the workload for you should be light, Forrest." There was more leeway with the summer staff, but if you were locked in, the station had to ensure the staff had their best chance.

"For now. Humans are social animals and we didn't evolve to live here for a reason. Anxiety and depression will set in for at least a third of the staff. Studies show lack of sun and natural vitamin D creation can induce symptoms of both, or exacerbate underlying conditions. Everyone here is an overachiever, so they may not realize or admit to the issue on medical forms."

Brilliant. Forrest was brilliant. Outlining issues impacting patients without coming off as a know-it-all. It was a skill many in their med school class had admired.

"There are a handful already diagnosed—"

"Myself included," Forrest interrupted. "I fought against the diagnosis when we—" He cleared his throat. At least Sam wasn't the only one having issues falling back on the body of knowledge they had on each other. "The point is that if anyone is struggling to admit it, I am more than willing to discuss my diagnosis and why it does not mean they are 'less than' in any way." Forrest nodded to the closet. "Medicine storage?"

"Yes. We're stocked well. Which is good, given that no help is coming for the next seven months." Sam walked over to the door and pressed his combination into the keypad. "I talked to IT. They're going to get you a code by the end of the day."

Forrest followed him in. "This looks like a closet, but wow, it's a small pharmacy."

"No." Sam shook his head. "I've worked in three hospitals that would have killed for this kind of setup. This is a small- to medium-sized pharmacy. Maybe even a true medium. Not that anyone actually has metrics for what counts for what." He was rambling. Words not fully making sense.

"Uh-huh." Forrest nodded, too polite to ask what the hell Sam was talking about.

"Everyday meds. Noncontrolled substances are here." Sam pointed to an area clearly marked. "The controlled substances are in back with another entry code. Most of them we shouldn't need. Unless we're performing surgery."

"Surgery? I am an internist who spends all his time in the lab." Forrest held up his hands, his eyes wide. "I haven't held a scalpel since residency."

Color was racing up his neck. He had always hated cutting into anyone. Which was a shame, because he'd have made an excellent surgeon. He was already a more than capable physician, but that didn't mean he enjoyed it. That was why Sam had known he'd never head into emergency medicine or surgery. Not that Forrest had ever questioned where he'd land, either. Internal medicine was all he'd wanted from day one of med school.

So why was he in a lab? At the South Pole!

"I hope it doesn't come to that, but I've done a handful of minor surgeries when no specialist was available. There was an elbow surgery overseen by video teleconference in a northern Alaskan outpost that was nerve-racking, but the patient is still going strong." His palms still sweated with the memory but Sam had managed and he could do it again, if absolutely necessary.

Forrest looked around the pharmacy then back at the door. "How is charting done here?" He opened the door and walked back out to the clinic area.

"It's standard charting. Like many facilities in the US, we use EPIC." Sam skirted around Forrest, who'd paused a little too close to the door when they'd exited. "But sometimes we have to use paper when the satellites are acting up."

"This is weird." Forrest shook his head and rocked back on his heels. "I know I'm the one who said we should act like colleagues just getting to know each other, but it's *weird*."

Sam shrugged, "It is. But we'll get through it. We are professionals."

"Professionals." Forrest didn't quite hide the scoff. "I mean, yes, of course we are."

"And you're my replacement, technically, not a teammate. I mean, you're likely going to have to work with me now and then, if the nurse practitioners need the night or day off, but really, we probably won't work together more than a handful of times."

A handful.

Probably fewer than a dozen. There wouldn't be a need.

Sam's soul sank. He needed to make up his mind. Either he was frustrated because he'd have to work with Forrest at all, or saddened by the fact that those occasions would be few and far between.

Can't have it both ways.

Forrest looked at him—really looked. "Are you all right?"

"Of course." It was mostly true. His life hadn't turned out like he thought it would but whose did? He'd done things he'd never dreamed of.

"Sam—"

"Any chance I can get an antibiotic cream? I scraped my hand on a machine and—" The young researcher stopped in the center of the room, and looked at the pair of them.

Sam had been so wrapped up in Forrest that he hadn't even heard her come in. "Sorry for your wait."

"I just got here." Her dark gaze rotated between him and Forrest. "If I'm interrupting, I can come back, it's just a scrape but—"

"No. We were done." Sam nodded to Forrest. "I'll let you know when we need you." Though he was going to do his absolute best to never need him.

"I guess we're done." Forrest swallowed and stepped past him and the researcher. Then he was gone.

It was fine. Fine. Everything was fine.

"You all right?" the researcher asked.

"Fine." The word bouncing around Sam's brain responded. "Let's get you some antibiotic cream." He had seven months left on the station. He'd done seven months or more in worse environments.

Not with Forrest.

CHAPTER TWO

Five days of silence from the clinic. Not that Forrest was tracking. He stared at the image on his electron microscope and tried to focus on the virus flourishing on the slide. This was why he was here. To study the effects of viruses in enclosed environments for space travel.

The idea was simple enough. If you brought in people, supplies and sealed off their location, no matter how cautious you were, millions of germs were going to hook a ride. But how fast did those germs mutate? How did they adapt? That was one of the millions of questions needing answers for long-term space travel.

That kind of space travel still lived in the realm of science fiction and Forrest doubted it would be achieved in his lifetime, but that didn't mean the research wasn't ongoing. And it benefited more than just space travel.

Bacterial and viral mutations were things that kept immunologists, epidemiologists and other doctors up at night. It was the basis for more than one of Forrest's own nightmares.

The phone rang and Forrest blinked as he looked at the contraption on the wall. It had rung exactly one other time while he'd been here. The only people who came to this lab were him and Charlee. Most contact was received via email—though the satellite-assisted internet connection meant it was hard to download attachments.

He picked up the phone, "Doctor Wilson. How can I help you?"

A cough echoed on the line, followed by the unpleasant sound of someone using a tissue. "I guess you holing up in the lab has one benefit." Charlee's voice was ragged. "You don't have the flu like half the post. Don't worry—"

Another coughing fit interrupted whatever Charlee was going to say.

"Half the post?"

"Yes. Good grief—get out of the lab. I guess that loader from the last supply flight wasn't right when he said it was 'just a cough.' Obviously not." Charlee started coughing again before taking what sounded like a sip of water. "And I've swabbed myself to preserve the specimen of whatever is making me feel like death." Another round of coughing.

"I'm not concerned about the swabs."

"Yes. You are." Charlee sighed. "It's what makes you so good at this. I'm taking at least today and tomorrow."

"Do *not* come back in here until you are completely better. And I do want the swabs. But it's more important that you get some rest. I will talk to you later."

Charlee hung up without saying anything else.

Yes, their research was important. Yes, they were on a limited schedule. But that did not mean Charlee needed to compromise her health.

And he *had* been in the lab basically nonstop since he'd visited the clinic.

Hiding.

He didn't enjoy admitting it, but if influenza was going around and Forrest hadn't even realized it, that meant he'd spent far too long in the lab. Sam and his team must be exhausted. But if they'd needed him, Sam would have rung.

No. He wouldn't.

Forrest had made it clear more than once that he was just the backup. That his research and lab came first. Those were the reasons he was here…but he was also a physician. One specializing in immunology and, to some extent, epidemiology. He might not have treated a patient in five years, but if there was an outbreak, he was still well suited to take care of the sick and then help ensure it didn't happen again.

And Sam didn't ring me.

That stung. But if the shoe had been on his foot, Forrest wasn't sure he'd have reached out, either. That wasn't a pleasant thought. He put the slides he was working on away and shut down the equipment. He was needed in the clinic. Whether Sam called or not.

It was a short walk. His quick pace was not the reason his heartbeat was echoing in his ears. He and Sam had worked side by side on so many shifts as med students. Sam excelling and Forrest doing his best to make sure no one saw how out of place he felt.

Then Sam had taken a residency in New York City and Forrest had gone to Seattle. As far away from the love of his life as possible. Hoping he'd feel like he belonged there.

There were coughs coming from the clinic and two patients were sitting on the bench outside the door. Forrest slid the mask he'd grabbed from his lab on. If influenza was making its way around the base, that meant it was a variant not receptive to the flu shot, because everyone on post had this season's vaccine before arriving. Enough people were sick; he didn't need to add himself to the ill population.

He stopped and did a quick triage. Each patient had a low-grade fever and dry cough.

"You're both sick, but not ill enough to be admitted to the clinic," he told them. "Go back to your rooms, take tea with honey for the cough and get as much sleep as you can manage." Like all medical doctors he'd done stints in the emergency room. When people felt terrible, they'd come in for reassurance that they'd be fine. At least it was a less expensive trip here than it would be in the States.

The virus needed to run its course. Unless someone's immune system was compromised, there was nothing but comfort care that the clinic could provide.

The two on the bench nodded, stood and slowly moved off.

"Come back if your fever is sustained at one hundred and three or higher."

They each raised a hand as he called out the final order.

The door of the clinic opened behind him and Forrest knew it was Sam. Just a few feet away. His heart rate picked up even more. His skin heated. The blood rushed to his face.

He turned. He was there to help. Whether Sam had called or not.

"Are you sending patients away?" Sam closed his eyes and opened them. Not a sign of frustration. Exhaustion clung to the physician. His eyes were hooded, his skin paler than normal and his lips were cracked. He was pushing himself to the edge.

"Are you the only one here?" Forrest pushed past Sam and shook his head. Two beds had occupants with IV drips. And no nurse practitioners visible.

Sam moved so he was on the other side of Forrest. Of course exhaustion wasn't slowing the former state champion rower down. "I asked a question first. Why are you sending patients away?" His arms were crossed and his eyes were fiery despite the exhaustion leaking from his pores. "Forrest—"

"They were running low-grade fevers and coughing. Classic influenza symptoms. I told them to drink tea with honey and get as much rest as possible. And to report back if their temperatures spike. This is a virus. There's nothing else we can do for them. Now—" he crossed his arms mimicking the man in front of him "—are you the only one here?"

Forrest knew the answer, but he needed the confirmation.

"Yes." Sam slid over to the desk and pulled up the tablet he used for charting.

To give himself something to do?

"Who were the two you sent back to their dorms?"

Sam was typing with one hand, no glint in his gray-blue gaze.

"I don't know. Two sick people who weren't sick enough to need more than rest and recovery time." Forrest shrugged. The offhanded movement was the wrong one.

Now Sam's gaze was full on boring into him. "What?" He held up a hand while shaking his head. "I know what you said. How could you not ask their names?"

"Again, what they needed was rest and maybe some cough drops, if we have them." Forrest's chest was hollow as he said the words. They were probably fine. That didn't change the fact that there were reasons you kept track.

Reasons he knew. Damn. He was rusty. And had made a mistake less than a minute in. Not a good start.

"And what if they get to their rooms and get too sick to call or come back? They need to be added to the infirmary's list." Sam ran a hand over his tired face.

It was a rookie mistake; one Forrest wouldn't have made if he'd worked with patients in the last five years.

"Sorry." He'd failed the first assignment. "I'll figure out who they were." Sam raised a brow but didn't point out that finding two patients when he didn't have more than a few seconds with each was a long shot.

Still. He'd find them. Records were important.

So much of the post was down with the flu that

accurate records might provide valuable information on who patient zero might be or how the virus was traveling so efficiently. And for that they needed to know everyone affected, time of sickness, severity.

"They'll probably be fine. Rest and fluids is all most need. But getting you out of your lab might have some benefits." Sam rolled his eyes then sat on the edge of the desk.

"How do you know I haven't been out? Keeping a check on me?" Those were questions he'd not needed to ask. Questions he didn't need answered.

Sam pinched the bridge of nose, then looked at the clock. "McMurdo Station is the largest research station in Antarctica but even at the height of its population there are a little over one thousand people here, and that's in the summer. Right now, there are two hundred and forty-seven. So a lone researcher who takes all his meals in his lab and sleeps there—"

"One time. And it wasn't sleeping, it was a nap."

Sam raised a brow, "You stand out, Forrest. Your absence stands out." He pushed himself off the desk, "Since you're here, I'm going to catch a quick nap. Natasha and Chris are both down with the flu, so it's just you and me."

"I'd have come sooner, if you'd called." Forrest said the words to Sam's retreating form. If the man heard them, he didn't react. If only Forrest could do the same.

Sam stared at the ceiling. Sleep had come—one did not work a decade plus in emergency medicine without learning to nap when and wherever you could. But that didn't mean his mind had settled.

The half-finished dreams had all revolved around Forrest. Replays of their life together. The horrid goodbye. The rudeness he'd projected earlier when Forrest had stopped in to help.

Rude was easy. It created a barrier. A wall. A case of ice around the heart he'd been forced to heal.

That didn't mean it was right.

And Forrest had had a point. Sam should have called. Should have notified his lab the second Chris went down. And certainly when Natasha developed a fever.

It was stubbornness that had kept him from reaching out.

And it was fear keeping him from swinging his legs over the bed and heading back to the clinic. It was late; Forrest needed a break. But now that Forrest knew Sam was working by himself, the man would insist on staying.

Forrest might have traded his clinician shoes for a lab coat but that didn't mean he'd sacrifice patient care. Sam had watched the color drain from his face when he'd asked for the names of the patients Forrest had sent away. Seen the realization that he'd failed to record the basics, and the shame. Known his former lover would beat himself up.

"No use holing up in here." Sam uttered the words to the empty room as he forced himself to get up and head to the clinic.

He slowly opened the door, slipping in before the

creak he'd noticed last week could echo in the quiet. The lights were turned down, probably to help the two individuals he'd admitted for IV fluids sleep.

Forrest looked up from the desk. Notes were strewn all over. The flashback to university, when Sam had labeled all his notes in a computer app and Forrest had piled notecards, sticky notes and sheets of paper everywhere, cut through Sam's heart.

This was why he'd avoided picking up the phone. Because every stupid little thing made him remember a life he'd spent years forgetting.

Apparently I didn't bury the memories far enough.

"Is there a reason you have papers everywhere?" Sam slid into the chair across from Forrest, waving off his unspoken offer of the primary desk chair.

Forrest held up a note and passed it to Sam. Two names.

Dr. Felix Lorraine, biologist.
Max Center, mechanic.

"How did you find them?" No explanation needed. These were the two Forrest had met in the hall. The two Sam had shamed him for.

Forrest turned the laptop around. Dr. Lorraine's and Max's badges were on the screen. Sam couldn't stop the smile on his lips. Searching the badge records was a unique way to find them. A very Forrest activity.

"I already reached out. They gave me the pertinent details. Both are still only running low-grade fevers and exhausted. Dr. Lorraine will stop by for cough drops later. I found the stash." Forrest rubbed his tense neck. "The two here are stable. I think they can be released to quarters tomorrow."

"Thank you." Sam sucked in a breath. "I should have called."

"You should have. But I understand why you didn't." Forrest turned the laptop back around. "However, I'm not leaving until one of the NPs is well enough to work with you."

Part of Sam rejoiced at the words. Not because he'd have qualified support but because Forrest was going to be here. With him. He needed to shut that feeling down. He could handle this himself. He'd worked by himself for years.

"I appreciate it, but—"

"Nope." Forrest's voice was low so as not to disturb the sleeping patients, "You're about to say that you've handled isolated conditions for years so you don't mind. *I* mind."

That was exactly what Sam had been about to say. Damn it. How were they both still so capable of reading the other?

"Why the remote locations?" Forrest crossed his arms. "Why are you here?"

They were repeats of the questions he'd asked five days ago. So Sam deflected with the same question he'd asked and gotten no answer to then. "Why are *you* hiding in a lab at the South Pole and not at the bedside? I seem to remember you loved figuring out what made people ill. And you were a master at it. The way you could read reports and see tiny differentials that stacked up to mean something all of us had seen one time on a med school test was one of the most impressive things I've ever seen. And now you're in a lab. Studying slides instead of healing the sick."

Forrest shifted, then met his gaze, "I had a patient—a little girl. Five. Sandy. She presented with a fever and UTI-like symptoms. And she worsened over the next few days, necrotizing enterocolitis. Every lab I saw, nothing made sense. It was cronobacter. The bacteria had gotten into her system from an herbal tea. It typically only affects newborns and the elderly. I never thought to check for it. By the time we figured it out—" Forrest shrugged.

How many times had Sam done that shrug after a hard shift in the ER? So many emotions carried on the up and down of shoulders. Only a medical professional who'd given the same shrug hundreds of times really understood the devastation hiding in such a little movement.

"The bacteria is rare. Only a handful of cases a year." Sam bit his lip to stop the words he knew wouldn't help. Statistics were comforting—when you or your loved one weren't creating the unlucky stat.

"At five, she should have had a better chance and if…" Forrest shook his head. "No use playing the if game."

That was something every doctor learned in med school. You could second-guess everything and the end result was still the same. It was a lovely platitude, but Sam had yet to meet a physician capable of truly abiding by it.

"Telling her parents broke me." Forrest spun the pen on the desk as his chest rose and fell with each word. "I failed at bedside. I wasn't able to do it."

He was in a prestigious lab in the South Pole working on foundational research. That was hardly what most people would label as failure. But it did sound like hiding.

Forrest didn't look up from the spinning pen. "The good thing about the lab is that the specimens are silent. Anonymous. Even when you look in the scope and see the worst-case scenario. It isn't my job to tell people that the person they love has less time than they thought. Or isn't coming home at all. Or that they are going to live, but won't ever be the same. I never start a sentence with *We did everything we could*."

The pen kept up its twirl, as Forrest's dark gaze hit Sam. "*That* is why I'm hiding in a lab. A failure to maintain my sanity at the bedside. Now, why are *you* here? Why are you traveling to remote locations and working alone?"

There was so much that Sam wanted to say. Rail against the idea that somehow Forrest was a failure. Tell him that if he was hiding then he wasn't where he was meant to be.

But fair was fair. Forrest had earned an answer of his own. However, admitting that he'd chosen constant traveling because both the men he'd planned to put down roots with hadn't wanted him would be less painful if one of those men wasn't sitting on the other side of the desk right now.

"I was engaged. Five years ago."

A twitch in Forrest's cheek was the only reaction to that statement.

What more was I hoping for?

Sam shrugged. Now he was the one hiding emotion in the simple action. "It's a freaking cliché story. Engaged, wedding less than a month away. I came home early from a shift because I was running a fever. Oliver was in bed with another man."

"Sam—"

"I don't want sympathy. I don't need it. My parents got the perfect union and I am never going to have it. No soulmate here. That's fine." There were days he almost believed the BS he was feeding himself.

Forrest cocked his head, "I wasn't planning on sympathy. I was going to say he sucked and didn't know what he had."

Sam waited for Forrest to look away. After all, the insinuation was Forrest hadn't known what he had, either. But Forrest didn't flinch. Sam rested his head in his hands.

"But how does a jackass ex-fiancé make you travel the…" His former best friend stopped and now it was pity coating his eyes. "You don't want to put down roots."

Not a question. Just a statement of fact. That damn long-term connection, still unbroken despite everything.

"Two men sitting at the ends of the earth who know they will never meet someone at the altar." If only Sam had a coffee cup to raise a mock toast with, preferably one that had a bit of an alcoholic kick to it.

Forrest looked at him. His hand was moving but before it reached Sam's he pulled back.

Sam didn't want his touch. Didn't need his comfort.

"I'm no longer sure I won't meet someone there." Forrest cleared his throat, "I think, well, older wiser and all that."

The irony.

"I feel like older, wiser me knows there is no point in exchanging vows. Weird how we flip-flopped." Where had this man been all those years ago? If Forrest had felt that way then, would they be celebrating their tenth wedding anniversary this year?

Yes.

Forrest wasn't the same man. But neither was he.

A moan from the door interrupted what was feeling a little too close to a pity party for Sam's liking.

Forrest was out his chair before Sam had turned around.

"Charlee? Charlee! I need you to keep your eyes open."

Forrest had barely left the lab. He knew Sam, the nurse practitioners and the people in his lab. Since Charlee wasn't a clinician, he suspected she had to be a member of Forrest's team.

"She's burning up." Forrest put one arm under her shoulder; Sam mimicked the action on the other side.

"Charlee, how much water have you had to drink?

Do you know what your temperature is?" The woman didn't answer Forrest's frantic questions.

"Forrest, get her to the bed." Charlee was dehydrated. The sunken eyes were a clear sign. A fact Forrest knew.

But when you were treating a colleague and a friend you could miss subtleties.

"Dizzy. Can't keep fluids." Charlee's breathless words echoed out as they laid her on the bed.

Sam pulled out his stethoscope. "Get the fluids while I listen to her lungs and heart."

Forrest moved immediately.

Unfortunately for Charlee, the nurses who could put in IV drips without even thinking were both down with the same virus taking its wrath out on her immune system.

"I haven't put an IV in since fourth year med school." Forrest set the bag of fluids on the stand.

"The good news is her lungs and heart sound good. I think the dizziness is dehydration. And I've done IVs when the ER was overloaded. I'm not as fast as the nursing staff, but we got this." Sam went to the sink, washed his hands and put on a pair of gloves. Then he started the IV.

With any luck, once Charlee was hydrated the worst of her symptoms would dissipate.

"Her temperature is one hundred and four." Forrest set the thermometer back on the counter by the bed. "Do we have liquid acetaminophen to push through her IV?"

"Yes." Charlee's fever was burning through the

fluids she had been able to take. They needed to get that temperature down otherwise the fever would consume the liquid from the IV, too.

Forrest headed for the med storage unit, reemerging a moment later with the tiny vial. The good news was that the IV push would get the fever suppressant directly into Charlee's bloodstream. Sam did the quick calculations, drew the syringe of meds and pushed it into the IV.

Forrest held up his hand, pressing a button on his brown watch. "It should start to work in five to ten minutes, if not then we need to push more."

"Let's focus on seeing if it comes down in five to ten." Sam swallowed as he stared at the watch—or where the watch was hidden under Forrest's long-sleeved scrubs. That was the watch Sam had given him on their third anniversary.

It was a simple piece. One bought when their funds were so tight they'd counted every penny. He'd saved for months.

It was a starter watch. One he'd planned to replace when they were settled. That day had never come.

But Forrest was more than capable of acquiring a better watch now. A fancier piece. A piece that screamed doctor, instead of drowning-under-med-school-debt student.

"Her fever's coming down." Forrest let out a sigh. "Thank goodness. Though she's still in for a long night."

Sam nodded, not trusting any words that might slip from his lips. He was in for a long night, too.

CHAPTER THREE

"You don't need to be here." Chris, one of the nurse practitioners on the station was looking much better today. He hadn't run a fever for three days, but yesterday he'd still looked rundown. "Nat and I can handle it. Get out of the clinic. Rest. Have fun. Do something."

He made a little shooing motion at Sam with his hands. It was juvenile but it made the point.

"Fine. I will go. But if either of you get too tired or need anything—"

"We won't." Natasha winked as she restocked the supplies next to the bed where Charlee had slept until this morning. The researcher wouldn't be joining Forrest in the lab for at least another few days, but Sam had released her to her quarters this morning. "Go."

Sam raised a hand and headed out of the clinic... to do what? The cafeteria didn't start serving lunch until eleven. He could head to his quarters, but there wasn't much to entertain him there. He was tired, but if he napped he ran the risk of messing up his sleep schedule.

What is Forrest doing?

This was the part of life he hated, the reason he did his best to keep moving. Because if he slowed down, his brain traveled places he didn't want to go.

His feet moved and before he knew it, Sam was standing outside Forrest and Charlee's lab. This wasn't where he'd meant to come. He wasn't really sure why he was here.

Still time to walk away. He probably should walk away. They'd spent most of the last three days working together in the clinic. There was no reason for Sam to just stop by.

But rather than retreat, Sam raised his hand and knocked.

"Come in, Sam." Forrest's voice was husky behind the door.

No turning back now. He turned the handle and stepped into the shockingly dark lab. "Is your head all right?" The man had been in the clinic for several days. Even if he was suffering a migraine, he'd show up just to ensure work got done. The man feared messing up more than anything. Or he had. It was why even though Forrest had been nearly perfect at bedside the last three days, he said more than once that wasn't accomplishing anything.

"My head is fine. You and I both seemed to avoid the Novel A Influenza strain circulating." Forrest turned the screen of the electron microscope around, showing off a beautiful image. "Weird how even viruses look pretty with enough magnification."

"You identified which flu strain took the base to nearly half capacity? How long have you been in here?" Forrest had signed off yesterday when Natasha had returned to the clinic full-time. Even if he'd showed up this morning, that didn't seem like enough time to fully work something like this out.

"I said it was *a* Novel A strain, not which one.

Those tests are still running, but I'll have an answer by the end of the day. It actually doesn't take as long to type them out as you think. The most important thing is to have enough samples to see any mutations." Forrest turned the electron scope back toward him.

"I have Charlee's samples and a few from the clinic. Charlee's is a mutated variant. Could explain why the virus hit her harder than others. I didn't get samples from the two others that had to have fluids, but there's a decent chance they had the same strain. The good news is that the mutated variant didn't seem as effective at spreading."

Sam crossed his arms, not frustrated, simply fascinated watching the man at work. "How do you know it wasn't as effective?"

"You and I are standing here." Forrest looked up from the screen and smiled. "We both moved Charlee from the door to the bed. Neither of us was masked. If it *was* as effective as the other strain, there's a good chance at least one of us would have the sniffles right now. If not the full-blown virus."

That smile was always what had fascinated Sam. Forrest could look at something most would ignore or push off as stuff other scientists or doctors did, and just dive right in. It was why no one had been surprised when he announced early in med school that he planning to go into internal medicine. And why no one was surprised he had never changed his mind.

He'd enjoyed the other specialties. Excelled at several of them. One of the neurosurgeons had practically begged him to consider brain surgery. Forrest had never budged. He'd known where he belonged.

Except he did change his mind.

He was locked away in a lab. Doing important research, but not serving patients directly. Patients he could truly help by being at bedside.

Forrest was amazing. He just never seemed to quite understand that fact.

"This whole situation made me realize I need to evaluate more samples," Forrest said. "People brought germs with them. They might not get ill from them, but others could be more susceptible. It's our own microcosm. So I've set up drop sites around the post with everything people need to give me daily samples. Voluntary, of course."

"Not sure you'll get daily samples." But he would get more than he had.

"Not planning on it. But I'll take what I can get. You aren't here to discuss that, though. What brings you to my lab?" Forrest tilted his head, "I doubt it was the flu strain. It doesn't much matter for the clinic what strain it is. Procedure is the same."

"I don't know." Such an honest answer. That was one the reasons he'd fallen for him. Seen forever with him. Forrest was easy to talk to. Easy to tell secrets to. Easy to love.

But he wasn't Sam's boyfriend any longer. Not the keeper of his secrets or his heart.

Forrest shut the electron microscope's screen off, pitching the already dark room into almost complete darkness. Then a light popped on. Sam squinted as his eyes adjusted.

"Sorry. I should have given some warning."

"It would have been nice." Sam blinked a few more times as his eyes screamed at the intrusion.

Forrest was by his side, not touching him, but so much closer than they'd been in the clinic. His scent, the soft pepper and cedarwood of the aftershave he'd used the entire time Sam knew him, wafted straight to his core.

A whole host of memories banged on the barricade Sam had erected around them. A not so solid wall these days.

The moment he'd given Forrest the watch slipped through. The expression on his face. The kiss they'd shared. The happiness that had felt like it would last forever.

"Why don't you have a new watch?" The question was pointless. Its answer mattered little in life's grand scheme.

"Watch?" Forrest's Adam's apple bobbed as he swallowed whatever he was going to say first. His right hand shifted, running over the piece still hiding on his left arm. "It's a good watch."

"No. It isn't." Sam chuckled as he slid back on his heels, putting a little more space between them. Millimeters, but millimeters that hopefully would keep him from acting any more rashly than he already was. "It was the best I could afford but it wasn't a good watch. It was—"

He wasn't sure where he was going or what the

pointless words could possibly lead to, so shut his mouth to trap any more inside.

His heartbeat pounded in his ears as the lab's silence radiated around them.

Say something.
Say something.
Say something.

He wasn't sure if his brain was chanting the words in hopes that Forrest's tongue would loosen or as an order to himself to add something to the quiet.

"Did you come because of the watch?"

There was a look in Forrest's eye. A hesitation? A question? A sorrow? Sam wasn't sure.

"Maybe. I saw it the other night. Seriously, why do you still have it? And don't say, it's a good watch. I got rid of everything." He cleared his throat. That was not what he'd meant to say. It wasn't even true.

His box of mementos was stuffed in the back of his closet at his parents' house. It had been carted from closet to closet at each of the locations he'd traveled to but when he'd signed up for this trip, he'd put everything back in his old room. And he'd taken the chance to rummage through the box again. Reliving the happiness, and the pain.

Movie tickets from their first date. The key from their first apartment. A Christmas ornament with them dressed as doctors he'd gotten for the holiday they'd never spent together. All things he should throw away.

There was no Oliver box. Sam really had thrown

those memories away. Rid his apartment, and his life, of the man.

But anytime he considered getting rid of the Forrest box, lifting the tiny thing felt like trying to carry the world. So it traveled with him. A piece of Forrest he couldn't cut away.

"I don't want to fight. We weren't very good at it anyway." Forrest wrapped his arms around himself, but he didn't step back.

"What does that mean? We weren't very good at it? Sure we were. We were civil and—" Sam closed his eyes. They had never really fought. They had spirited discussions. But never true arguments.

He'd always thought they were so in tune with each other there was no need to argue. Until Forrest walked away. Then he'd wondered if they'd avoided arguing because they were hiding things from each other. Except Sam hadn't hidden anything. He'd made sure Forrest knew the future he saw for them. Forrest had hidden the fact that he didn't see that future.

"Part of me hates that you're here." Sam bit his lip. "Sorry. That was mean and cruel."

"But honest." Forrest let out a sigh. "So you came to say your piece. It wasn't possible in the clinic. Even with the patients sleeping, we weren't alone."

He gestured with a hand then wrapped his arm back around himself. "Say what you need to say, Sam."

"Why are you still wearing a watch that a lover *you* walked away from gave you?" That was the part that tore at Sam. He had seen no cracks in their love.

No pain. He'd believed Forrest was his person. The other half of his soul. He planned their future while Forrest was planning to walk away, shattering his soul and cratering the life he'd planned.

Yet, the man had kept the love token.

He looked at Forrest's wrist. "Why?"

Emotions clogged his throat. Damn him. Sam had done a half-decent job of keeping his feelings in check, at least around Forrest. He made sure the dirt he laid over the grave in his heart never shifted. And then a stupid watch had undone everything.

And Forrest had just gone to his lab. Restarted his day. Followed his routine. Picked up and restarted without any issues. Like he had all those years ago.

He was the one that walked away. What did you expect?

"I didn't want to get rid of it." Forrest's thumb ran along his wrist, feeling the face of the watch under his sweater. "I didn't throw everything away."

"Just the most important part, right? Me." Shit. That wasn't helpful. To him or Forrest.

"Are you mad at me and a watch or your ex-fiancé? The one that made you run from the life you planned? I can handle anger, Sam, I just need to know who you are really cursing." Forrest tilted his head, such a methodical reaction.

The man had always kept his cool in frustrating times. Never raised his voice. Never thrown hands. Never called someone a name. It was a trait Sam had admired until Forrest had used it to walk away from him.

Until Forrest had told them they were done in the same cool tone. No emotion. No fire. No tears. Just a cold hard truth.

Coming here was a mistake. One he needed to rectify. "I am fine with my life."

"You wouldn't be pissed at the watch I'm wearing if that was true."

Forrest and his damn insights.

"I apologize for coming." This wasn't the way to spend his time off. He'd barged in and made an ass of himself. Not the standard he held himself to. "I hope you get whatever answers you're looking for in there." Sam gestured to the electron microscope then turned on his heel.

He needed to be anywhere else.

Now.

It took longer to shut down the lab equipment when Forrest was the only one there. Plus there had been tests he needed to complete before cleaning everything up for the day. But he'd managed it as quickly as possible.

Sam was struggling. It was terrifying.

The man had always been in control. Perfect. A former state champion rower who had turned down a chance at the Olympics because it would impact his start date at university. His nearly perfect scores on tests had infuriated and impressed their friends.

He was always collected. Hell, even with the influenza outbreak he'd held it all together. If Charlee hadn't called in sick, alerting Forrest to the outbreak, Sam would have handled it all on his own.

But years of therapy had unlocked the knowledge that just because you were functioning on the outside, didn't mean the internal wasn't twisted unrecognizably.

Forrest closed and locked the lab then headed to Sam's quarters. He ran his hand along the watch that had inflamed the interaction. He'd kept it for a simple reason.

It reminded him of a time in his life that was nearly perfect. The one time in his life he'd known love.

He'd grown up under the ever-watchful eye of his grandmother. Her cutting remarks had been a constant reminder that he was a mistake. His mother had never shared his father's identity, if she'd even known who he was.

She'd dropped Forrest at his grandmother's door when he was less than a week old. The only thing he could credit his grandmother with was that she hadn't turned him over to the system.

He'd met Sam as an undergrad. Loved him as a med student. Walked away right before residency so the man had the chance at something better than the broken man he slept beside every evening. The man who might be top of his class but felt completely out of place. The man who internally cringed whenever marriage was brought up because he was certain he'd make a terrible spouse. Forrest had grown up in a home without that kind of love and was terrified he'd mess everything up eventually.

And instead of finding what he had wanted, Sam was hiding in rural locations, moving from place to place, not staying long enough to form real connections. It was clear he needed a friend, whether he was willing to admit it or not.

And Forrest was going to oblige. Or force his way in. Somewhere, Sam had lost sight of how wonderful he was. Put away the dreams he'd always wanted. Forrest hadn't been lying when he'd said the ex-fiancé hadn't known what he had.

His fists were clenched, and Forrest took a breath as he unclenched them. He was furious at a man he'd never met.

And jealous as hell.

Burning poured across his chest. The man, Oliver, could have had the world. And he'd thrown it away.

And destroyed a man Forrest would always care about.

Forrest reached the door of Sam's quarters and knocked on it. He waited a minute, but there was no response. So he knocked again.

"Go away, Forrest. I am fine."

So Forrest wasn't the only one who knew when the other one was standing on the wrong side of a door.

He grabbed the handle and walked in. The good news was that, in the winter, with so few people at the pole, most people didn't have a roommate. Forrest himself was currently using the extra bed in his room to store the clean clothes he kept meaning to put away.

"Hey!" Sam's mouth was hanging open as he stared at Forrest.

Forrest closed the door behind him and moved to sit on the extra chair in the little seating area Sam had set up. Like him, Sam was living in a double room with no additional partner.

He took the watch off and tossed it on the table between them. "Do you want it back?"

"Don't be ridiculous." Sam leaned back, trying to put as much distance between them in the small room as possible.

It stung. But Forrest wasn't going to give in to that feeling now. There'd be plenty of time to wallow when he was in his own room.

He gathered the watch and slid it back onto his wrist. Then he crossed a leg over his knee and put his arms on the back of the chair. He'd stay until Sam physically removed him or started talking.

Sam's gaze held his. His chin raised. Challenge set. "It's not fair."

"Little in life is. But what exactly do you mean this time?" Forrest's stomach twisted and he prayed the uncertainty raging through him wasn't clear on his face. He was here for Sam right now. Not himself.

Sam took a deep breath and rolled his head from one side to the other. "I said we should be colleagues. Act like none of the history is there. I'm the one who suggested it. And yet—" he flung his hand out at Forrest "—you are the one unconcerned by it and I'm pissed at a watch."

Forrest wasn't unaffected. His stomach tumbled

right now, just to prove that point. "I think you're pissed because I'm a reminder that you didn't get the life you planned. You're in one of the most interesting places in the world. A place you could convince yourself was the plan...if I wasn't here."

Sam cleared his throat. "I always hated how you could look at something and just get right to the point."

Forrest had never felt like he had that skill. He was just quiet. Saw more than most because he wasn't attempting to control conversations. Most physicians he knew were extroverts. There was nothing wrong with that, but it meant that in many conversations they were waiting to say something, rather than fully listening.

It occasionally caused a problem when doctors figured they knew what was going on without really listening to their patients' concerns.

"We were friends for a long time. I think enough time has passed that we could be again. I know you're stinging from the end of your engagement..."

"My engagement ended five years ago." Sam bit his lip like that was the last thing he'd wanted to say. "You're right. You are a reminder of a different life plan. One I thought I had buried when I found Oliver. But none of that's your fault."

"You need a friend." Forrest knew Sam was about to kick him out. About to tell him to get lost. And that was fair. After all, he'd ended things between them. But the man was an extrovert by nature. And just like Forrest had holed up in the lab, Sam was doing the exact same thing.

Except he was holing up in locations he knew he wasn't staying in. Everyone was transient in his life. So no real connection. No heartfelt goodbyes. No life plan to mess up.

"A friend who cares and will listen to whatever. And who actually knows you."

"Volunteering?" Sam laughed but there was no humor in the sound.

"Yes." Forrest forced the emotions clawing their way up his throat down. Sam was important and the man was doubting himself, whether he wanted to admit that or not.

He deserved a happy home. He could have that as a traveling physician, with the right partner. Or he could chase the dream that Forrest suspected was still in his heart.

A stable home. A long career at a top trauma unit. A family to come home to every evening. He was getting a later start on it than planned, but it could still be his. If he opened himself up.

"We are good friends. Or we were." Forrest held up his hand. "We were always able to have conversations and laugh before—" he hesitated for only a moment before continuing "—before we took it to a different place. We have this Antarctic winter for you to come back out of the shell you've retreated into since you started traveling. Think of me as practice for when you get back to the real world, if you need to."

"And if I don't want a friend?" Sam raised his chin, but Forrest could see the indecision in his eyes.

"You do. And I need to get out of the lab. We can do this." Forrest was nearly sure of it. "We'll both be better for it."

"Fine."

Not a ringing endorsement, but a start.

CHAPTER FOUR

Sam considered calling things off and hiding in his suite all day. He looked at the phone and shook his head. What was the point? Forrest had already barged in once.

Friends.

He'd agreed to be friends—with Forrest. Maybe he needed his head examined, because this had disaster written all over it.

But hiding away wasn't fixing anything, either. And there was part of him that missed his friendship with Forrest. Before they'd been lovers, he'd been the one Sam turned to with everything.

This era of their friendship would not be like that one. Forrest was right about one thing. Sam was lonely.

Had been lonely for so long.

He'd swoop into a place, serve the three or six or even nine months that was on his contract. He'd be friendly with the locals but did not make friends. Did not plan out his life or try to find forever.

Grabbing the light jacket off the hook, Sam opened his door—and paused.

Forrest raised a hand. "Morning."

"Wha—" Sam couldn't even finish the word.

Forrest shrugged and put his hands in his pockets. "I thought you might be second-guessing this and trying to avoid breakfast."

"I considered it." Sam matched Forrest's shrug as

he closed the door to his room and pulled on his coat. Their dorms weren't located in Building 155, the main facility at McMurdo Station. There were lines between the buildings you could hold on to to make sure you got where you needed to go. Today it was still bright enough that they didn't need them.

They marched across the way and walked into the canteen. Grabbed their trays and breakfast. All without saying a word.

A group of mechanics stood up and cleared out a table. Forrest slid into the recently vacated chairs and Sam followed.

"Did you sleep all right?" Forrest grabbed a banana from his tray and tore open the peel. The bananas grown in the hydroponic farm on the station were a dwarf variety and tasted slightly different from the ones you got at home. But on the days when you got "freshies," the nickname people gave fresh fruit and veggies grown or flown into the station, you enjoyed the prized commodities.

"I slept fine." Sam did not hide the yawn the question seemed to call from his soul.

Forrest raised a brow but didn't push. "I have a colleague studying sleep patterns in a confined environment. He put in for a stint down here but wasn't approved."

"There's always next year." Sam wasn't a scientist, but he knew getting lab or research space in Antarctica was a prize most never achieved. It was impressive that Forrest was "hiding" here.

Forrest nodded as he dumped more than a healthy amount of brown sugar in his oatmeal.

"You know they serve this buffet style. There are a ton of options. You aren't required to eat oatmeal." A smile pulled at the corner of Sam's lips.

An old running joke.

To cover a painful childhood when all Forrest was permitted for breakfast was bland oatmeal.

"I like oatmeal."

"You like—" Sam held up two of the four empty packets of sugar "—brown sugar."

Forrest smiled and looked at the overly sweetened breakfast. "I like oatmeal. *With* brown sugar."

He took a big bite of the meal and put a ridiculous smile on his face. The over-the-top dramatics were funny and Sam couldn't contain the chuckle that slipped out.

It felt weird and somehow not, to be joking and laughing. This was Forrest. His soul knew this man. Recognized him. Enjoyed spending time with him.

"So where are you based at these days?" Forrest took another bite of oatmeal. Maybe determined to finish the meal to prove a point.

"You picked me up from my room." Sam cleared his throat. That sounded a little too much like this was a date. "You know where I'm based."

"Very funny." Forrest pointed the spoon at him. "You move all the time, but where are you based? Where are you heading back to after this?"

Sam shrugged. It was a question his mother asked him far too often.

Where to next, Sam? Is there a plan? A point to the journey?

The worry in her eyes always made him fidget. And he fought the urge to do the same now.

"That is a problem for future Sam. I've put feelers out to places, but no final destination in mind." He winked and managed not to look away when Forrest raised his eyebrow. "And you? Where is home now?"

"Indiana."

"Indianapolis?" There was a huge pharmaceutical company there. One known for their research throughout the world. But that didn't tally with Forrest's posting in Antarctica, examining remote locations and viral modifications in small populations. That wasn't something the company studied.

Or maybe it was.

Sam had never investigated the company himself. His interactions had been limited to the sales reps that showed up at clinics far too often.

"Yeah. Indianapolis." Forrest nodded, "But the research here is government based. A contract." He set his spoon down, all the oatmeal gone. "Been there for about five years. It's a nice enough place."

Such a glowing recommendation.

That meant Forrest had completed his residency and spent less than two full years at bedside. Those early years on the wards could be tough. It would be easy for the Forrest Sam had known to see any mess up as a reason to run. Perhaps this friendship could remind Forrest why he'd gone to med school in the first place—to work with patients.

"Anyone waiting for you at home?" Jobs, weather, family. Such bland topics. Except this question cut to Sam's core. He wanted Forrest happy.

He'd mentioned he was open to the idea of marriage now. Was it because he'd met someone that had made him realize it was for him?

Someone better than me.

"No." Forrest laughed but there was discomfort layered under it. "I am perpetually single." He pursed his lips before looking at the door. "What do you do for entertainment these days? Do you still go to opening nights for huge movies, even if you don't know much about the fandom?" Forrest's dark gaze hit him.

"Nope." Sam had stopped that not long after residency started. Used residency as an excuse. After all, he'd always gone by himself most of the time. Forrest hadn't had the money for many extras. Even when they'd started dating, it had been rare they were both free on a Thursday or Friday night.

But with no one to come home and tell about the experience, what was the point?

"Ah," Forrest said. "I went to the last major superhero opening. Got to see everyone in costumes. I hadn't seen all the movies though, so I missed some of the subplots. But the special effects were unbelievable. As was the storyline about a virus turning someone into a supervillain."

"I didn't see any of those." Sam had meant to. And he'd bluffed his way through a conversation about them more than once with a young patient who came into the ER needing distraction from a broken bone, or other ailment. But Oliver had scoffed at seeing the first one with him and Sam hadn't argued because he wanted the man happy. He'd always wondered if he could have found ways to make Forrest happy if he'd stayed. Except Forrest had never *seemed* unhappy with their relationship until it ended, while Oliver had never been silent regarding any slight, perceived or real.

When the engagement ended the series had been several movies in and Sam had never gotten around to seeing them alone.

"Wow." Forrest took a deep breath. "Do you still cook?" He waited a minute and shook his head. "No, because for one person what is the point? That used to be my line."

"Doesn't make it untrue." Once upon a time Sam had taken pride in the meals he created. Most of them had worked, but the terrible mistakes had been highlights, too. "I'm pretty rusty on friend talk."

Forrest grabbed his juice and drank it down. "Guess it's a good thing we still have most of the winter to unlock you then." He gave Sam a wink but red was creeping up his neck.

At least Sam wasn't the only one struggling with this.

"I was planning to stop by the clinic today. Just to check in on stuff. Stay up-to-date in case you need anything from me."

Work talk. That was something Sam was good at. In fact it was pretty much the only type of conversation he'd had since his engagement ended.

Now, that was a sad thought.

"Good idea." His throat was tight, but he managed to push out a question—after all, why should Forrest ask nearly all of them? "You still play the guitar?"

He'd gotten him one for Christmas when they were college roommates, after Forrest discussed how much he'd always wanted to learn. Had he thrown it away after they'd broken up?

"Yes. I brought one. It's in my room. Luckily there's no way I will annoy a roommate with my skills."

"Annoy? You were good at it. Do you not practice at all? Or are you just denigrating your talents?" It was the second one. Forrest never gave himself enough credit.

He stuck his tongue out at Sam. "I still prefer pop songs and they're not everyone's favorite. That's what I meant by annoy my roommate."

"Uh-huh." Now it was Sam's turn to raise his eyebrow. His chest loosened as Forrest playfully shook his head at him.

"The *point*..." Forrest pointed the spoon at him "...is yes. I still have the guitar. I even have an electric one, a bass guitar, and a drum set. The drums get no use. I bought them on a whim. Probably because my grandmother would have hated the bright red noisy thing. I keep thinking I will sell the set, but then I keep it—despite the fact that I can't keep time on it at all!"

"You can't keep time? Of course you can. You play guitar. You have great hands. I mean Dr. Poled wanted you to be a neurosurgeon so bad." Sam raised his hand. "Come on, Forrest."

"Keeping time for my guitar or the bass is *not* the same. I mean, you're supposed to hit multiple different drums or cymbals with different timing. I was steady in the surgical suite. That's not the same thing as keeping time. And Dr. Poled wanted me to go neuro because I was one of the only ones who excelled in it who wasn't an asshole. She hated the others, and I can't say that I blamed her."

"That field does have more than its fair share of people with God complexes. I think it's a necessity given that they are cutting into people's brains—literally."

"God complex or not, there's no reason to act like a jerk." Forrest grabbed his plate. "We need to get going."

Sam picked his tray up, too. It was time to go, but somehow in the space of half an hour they'd gone from awkward as hell to pseudo-normal.

And he'd enjoyed it.

Forrest looked over the selection of DVDs in the community room. He hadn't watched a DVD in forever, but the station's internet was reserved for research and contact with home. So people brought DVDs and left them here for others to enjoy when they had downtime.

He'd brought a handful of movies himself, but with the exception of a foreign film he loved, they were all repeats of the ones already here.

"Find anything good?"

Forrest didn't jump at Sam's voice. That was positive. Over the last week they'd eaten nearly every meal together. He'd stopped by the clinic a handful of times.

They were acting closer to friends. Sure, the ease they'd had once upon a time was gone. But then they weren't those people anymore. Too much had happened to the men they'd been to go on the same way.

Plus, the mild awkwardness that remained was a good reminder that the time on the ice was temporary.

"Find anything?" Sam repeated the question and slid up next to him to look at the stack. He smelled like fresh-cut grass.

So he still used the same soap. Forrest could practically see the green bar. A horrid color that stained the shower wall. But the smell was so perfect, Sam said it was worth it.

It is.

"Do I have to ask a third time? If you don't want to do movie night—"

"I want to do movie night," Forrest interrupted. "I just don't know what to select. I mean, 'anything good' means so many different things to different people."

And there would be others here tonight. Sam had said he was bringing the popcorn. Charlee was planning to hang out and Chris, one of the NPs for the clinic, had said he'd stop by. What movie should he select for a group like that? A rom-com? A comedy? Horror?

Not horror. There was a reason that stack was collecting dust on the side.

And not a superhero flick. That might alert Sam to the fact that Forrest was spending far too much of his time remembering every word he had said over the last few days.

"It's just a movie, Forrest." Sam squatted down next to him. His body so close. If either of them turned their head, their lips would—

Shut it down, Forrest.

During the week they'd spent eating breakfast and dinner together, his brain had brought forth all the old feelings. The ones that had never gone anywhere. He'd still loved Sam when he'd ended things, just wanted more for him.

Sam deserved the world. And he hadn't taken it.

"I know. But Charlee likes documentaries, Chris mentioned comedies, you like superheroes—or you did."

Sam laid his hand against Forrest's shoulder. "You're in charge of movie night tonight. That means you get to choose what you like."

Forrest rolled his eyes. If he wanted a crowd-pleaser, following his own taste was the worst way to find one. He'd only watched the one superhero movie he had seen because so many lab techs had been talking about it. Not because he'd really wanted to see it. "What *I* like is documentaries that the person standing next to me has repeatedly remarked are depressing." He focused on the collection. What was the right answer?

"You liking depressing documentaries was surprising. Given how you grew up, I was always stunned you didn't stick to happy films. Fluff." Sam squeezed Forrest's shoulder then moved his hand.

The ghost of the touch lay heavy on Forrest's heart.

Sam pulled back, a little. "There isn't a wrong answer."

"I know." Forrest let out a sigh as his gaze hovered on the selection.

"Do you?" Sam's hand started back toward him.

Forrest couldn't let him touch him again. The touches were comfort. Meaningless moments that his heart saw as anchors. He grabbed a movie and pulled out of Sam's reach.

"This one." He handed it to Sam hoping Sam wouldn't ask what movie he'd chosen because he didn't know.

Sam looked at the movie, pursed his lips and headed over to the player.

"What are we watching?" Charlee rounded the corner.

"Ever After." Sam held up the DVD of the Cinderella retelling.

Forrest knew the movie. Their suite mate in sophomore year had had a girlfriend that had watched it over and over again during finals week. She had sworn the Drew Barrymore movie was the best Cinderella story ever.

And I just grabbed it from the stack.

"Fun choice." Charlee grinned. "A fish may love a bird but where would they live."

Sam clapped. "She can quote the movie just like…" He put his hand on his chin and scrunched up his nose. "What was Dan's girlfriend's name? The one that had this on replay?"

"Rebecca." They'd married right after graduation. Forrest and Sam had danced together all night at their reception. Another good memory. His brain seemed incapable of keeping them buried.

"Oh. You guys went to college together?" Charlee grabbed one of the bags of popcorn and dumped some into the bowl she'd brought, then took a seat in one of the only single chairs.

"We lived together all through med school." Sam poured popcorn into his own bowl and took the other chair. At least they wouldn't be crammed together on the couch all night.

"Who lived together? Oh, popcorn!" Chris had entered. He grabbed a bowl too and put a healthy amount of popcorn in it. "Now, who lived together? I love gossip."

"It's not gossip." Forrest shook his head. "Sam and I were freshman roommates, then we lived together through med school. He got an ER residency at the top trauma unit in New York City and I was sent to Seattle to work in immunology."

"You chose Seattle." Sam threw a piece of popcorn into his mouth. "It was a choice. Not a *sent*. You were their top pick and they were yours."

Forrest saw Charlee turn her gaze toward him but

he wasn't going to say anything. After all, Sam was right. He'd listed Seattle first on his match list. The way the US medical system worked, the match was binding. But the truth was that every hospital program he'd listed was on the West Coast.

And he'd known that Sam had been planning to put several New York–based hospitals on his list. Given Sam's expertise, Forrest had known he'd end up at the other end of the country. And hopefully find someone there that had a plan. Someone who felt like they belonged in their chosen world, rather than someone like Forrest. An imposter. A person wearing a mask, acting like they'd found their place.

At the time stepping out of the way had seemed like a worthwhile sacrifice. Now he wasn't so sure.

"You two knew each other in college, stayed in touch and both ended up on the winter rotation here. That is so cool." Chris grabbed a fistful of popcorn and started munching.

They hadn't stayed in touch, but neither man spoke up. Thank goodness. Because if Chris really loved gossip, then that fact was bound to prick his interest.

"Movie time." Forrest grabbed the remote and pushed Play.

The title screen appeared along with music his brain could replay from memory.

Sam's hip buzzed.

"What's up?" Forrest pushed the pause button. "Does Nat need help?" The nurse practitioner was the only one on duty at the clinic tonight. Technically, the station called it a hospital, but the building was too small for Forrest to think of it that way.

"There was an accident in the motor pool. Several mechanics need stitching up." Sam frowned as he put his popcorn on the table. "There are at least four coming in."

"What the hell were they doing?" Chris groaned as he set his popcorn bowl down. "I was looking forward to movie night."

"Stay." Forrest hadn't even gotten popcorn for himself yet. "I'll help patch them up. Enjoy your evening."

Chris wasn't interested in arguing. "Thanks."

Forrest waited until he and Sam were out of hearing range. "I wanted you to have the life you wanted. The perfect family you dreamed of. That was why I went to Seattle."

"And yet we're both here. At the end of the world. Alone." Sam pulled on his coat and stepped out into the cold.

CHAPTER FIVE

THE LAB WAS quiet this morning. That was the way Forrest liked it. No questions. No judgment. His own little hidey-hole.

The lab he worked in back home had ten stations and unless he came in around five the noise level was always pretty high. Not because people weren't working but because the everyday movements of twelve or so people added up.

Today he'd walked to the lab around four. When it had become apparent that he wasn't going to sleep. Charlee was a late arrival person. That meant he had until at least nine on his own.

Coward.

He'd skipped breakfast. Or rather he was currently skipping breakfast. He and Sam had met in the canteen every day for the last week at six thirty. Usually they were the first and second people to grab food.

It had become a routine he enjoyed. Maybe too much.

Last night he and Sam had patched up the mechanics—who'd bet each other they could slide farther on the patch of ice out their door. All four of them had made it around the same distance and ended up with stitches in their legs, hands or both from the sharp ice.

A lesson learned. Maybe.

Antarctica was amazing. But the winter was also long and dark, and boredom set in easily.

Forrest would have liked to pretend boredom was why he wanted to march out of the lab right now and see if Sam was still eating breakfast. He might be hiding in the lab but he wasn't lying to himself. He liked hanging out with Sam. Loved it. It made him feel whole for the first time in a long time.

The lab door opened and Sam walked in. "I figured you might be hungry." He set the to-go box on the desk by the front door. "I even put a container of oatmeal in there and five packets of brown sugar."

"I don't need five packets." Forrest stuck his tongue out and walked over to the food. "Four is plenty."

Sam grinned and put his hands in his pockets. "Sorry about what I said last night."

Forrest just nodded. He hadn't been wrong. They were both at the end of the world—alone.

"I feel like one of us is always apologizing and I feel like it's usually me." He let out a breath. "I missed you and there's still part of me that's pushing you away."

Forrest opened the box. Four packets of brown sugar sat next to the oatmeal. The exact right amount.

"The extra one is in my pocket." Sam pulled the little packet out. "Just in case."

"Thanks." Forrest got the oatmeal ready. "I was actually just thinking about stopping down there for food."

Sam nodded. "I figured you were working. Now that I'm here, I'm realizing I never asked." He coughed and looked down before meeting Forrest's gaze, "What *are* you working on in here while you're hiding? I mean, you said immunology in isolation, but I honestly have no idea what that means. I thought your company worked on new prescription drugs."

Forrest understood why he hadn't asked. Other than his admission of why he'd swapped the bedside for lab work and Sam's acknowledgment of his failed engagement, they'd kept the conversation topics light.

He took a bite of the sausage Sam had added to his breakfast. Swallowing, he pointed to the electron microscope. "They do work on drugs, but also on other government and private projects. Plus the information gleaned from this could benefit new drug development. But the focus here is viral load changes in small populations. It's a major concern for space travel. And things like long submarine stints, even research stations like this. In theory, fewer people equals fewer germs and fewer chances for a virus to mutate. However, no matter how careful you are, germs are coming into your environment. So, what if one mutates and is able to run through the whole population, or close to it?"

Sam crossed his arms, tilting his head, but he didn't say anything.

So Forrest continued, "On a submarine, you could surface and get aid. At the station, we have meds and can self-isolate. But what about on a space station? Or on a rocket to Mars? On a Martian outpost? For humans to have successful space flight, we have to understand the immunology changes that happen. How do our immune systems change in isolation?"

"You think we will have an outpost on Mars?"

Forrest chuckled. Sam wasn't the first person to ask that question about his research. "I doubt it. At least not in our lifetimes. But eventually? Maybe. Humans are curious creatures. We want to explore. The earth is known. At least that's what people will tell you. I think there are still so many mysteries to discover and solve."

"Research with an outcome you won't see." Sam shook his head. "I don't think I could do it. I want answers. Now."

"That isn't true. You live in a world of uncertainty in the emergency room." Forrest finished off the oatmeal and put the trash in the special container every room had. Everything that entered the station was taken off. Nothing was left. It was an interesting program designed to protect the South Pole as much as possible.

"No. That isn't true. I know what the outcomes are."

"But you don't." Forrest had seen it so many times during the med school emergency room rotation. During every rotation. "Everyone thinks doctors have all the answers. Hell, even some doctors think we have all the answers. That with enough tests, enough scans, enough something, we will unlock whatever the mystery is."

"I am not talking about internal medicine or neuro or some other unique specialty, Forrest. I know there aren't enough tests sometimes." Sam's fingers were clenched on his arms. His shoulders tight.

Forrest reached over, pulled a hand loose. The connection burned as he forced Sam to relax. "What happens to the patient when they leave your emergency room? When the car crash victim gets home, when the drunk who dented their head detoxes and heads out, when the teen boy who broke his arm jumping from the roof into the pool gets another wild idea?"

"That's different." Sam flexed the hand Forrest had touched, then released it.

"How?" Forrest looked at the lab he enjoyed so much. "I know that I'm making a difference. But exactly what that difference is? No human can truly know that. Your job is to stabilize people. Then they move on. Hopefully, you provide something that will stick with them."

He shrugged as Sam looked toward the lab. He'd done a rotation in the ER. Patients cycled in and out. Some came in so often the staff knew more about them than their friends or family. Others came once and you never saw them again.

"What's the coolest thing you've seen in that microscope?" Sam's words were barely audible.

Whether he meant to ask the question or not, Forrest knew the answer. "Yersinia pestis."

Sam's head swung back toward him. The man's perfect mouth was hanging open. "Black death. Your answer is the black death?"

"It's the bacteria responsible for the plague. I studied under the scientist that basically confirmed the bacteria was responsible for wiping out more than half of the European population."

Forrest stood and grabbed Sam's hand as he pulled him toward the lab.

"If you have that bacteria here, I do not want to see it." Sam chuckled but he didn't let go.

"I don't." He turned the microscope on, and pulled a slide onto the deck, a little awkwardly since his hand was still holding Sam's.

"This is the virus that took out the station." He pointed to the edge of the virus. At magnification of one hundred thousand, the virus was well defined.

Sam dropped his hand but he didn't step away.

"Charlee's virus looks different in the edges from the other samples. That is where the mutation happened." He pulled the slide out and slid the one with Charlee's sample on it. He gestured to the same edge. "See the difference here?"

"No." Sam tilted his head. "But I don't need to." He took a step closer.

He's just getting a better look at the microscope.

His scent filled Forrest's lungs. Sam. His heartbeat pounded in his ears as he stared at the only man he'd ever loved. The only person who'd loved his flawed self.

"Never forget—" Sam didn't look at the microscope; his gaze was rooted on Forrest "—just how smart you are. A genius."

"Hardly," Forrest scoffed, "I left the bedside and had to do something to pay the bills. These are influenza samples, if you looked, you'd see—"

Sam's finger was laid over his lips.

Whatever he'd been about to say evaporated from

Forrest's tongue. All he could focus on was the gray-blue tones in the eyes holding him.

"You are brilliant." Sam took a deep breath and pulled his hand away.

There were no words coming to mind. Nothing but the two of them. The tiny space between them burned.

Sam's lips were so close, the moment frozen. Sam leaned closer.

The door to the lab opened and Charlee entered, letting out a sigh.

Sam jumped back, whatever the moment was about to be gone in an instant.

"I swear Mondays are terrible no matter where you are in the world. Even at the end of it." Charlee hung her coat on the hook by the door before finally recognizing that Sam was in the lab standing next to Forrest.

"Doctor Miller? Is Forrest boring you with the tiny hook difference on my sample? It *is* there. But you have to look really close. Really, really close." She laughed and winked at Forrest. "Only he would spot it. Though he won't take credit."

"It's not boring. I am not surprised by the credit thing, though." Sam cut Forrest a look before taking another step back. " I should head to the clinic."

"Thanks for bringing breakfast. I appreciate it." Forrest swallowed his desire and the dozens of questions pooling in his brain.

"You're welcome but it was a one-time thing. Tomorrow, eat in the canteen. Time away from here is good, too."

"Hear, hear." Charlee offered Sam a high five which he took as he headed out the door. "I like him."

"Yeah." Forrest nodded and turned his focus back to the microscope. They'd nearly kissed. That was where the moment was leading. Wasn't it?

Forrest ran a finger over his lips then shook his head. As if that would force the thoughts of Sam loose, thoughts that had lodged there since he'd seen him on the ship.

"Maybe you should ask him out? You guys seem to get on well."

He was not discussing Sam. Not with Charlee or anyone else. Forrest pointed to the edge of the virus. "It's a tiny adjustment, but it is important. This was likely what made you so ill, and the hook may be why it wasn't as capable of spreading. Hardly boring."

Charlee tilted her head. "Okay, I get the point. No personal talk."

He'd nearly kissed Forrest. That was where the moment was leading yesterday. Sam had stood in the lab fascinated by the impressive work his former love was doing.

How Forrest could consider his life path a failure was beyond him. Maybe he thought that because he missed bedside. He'd been great at it. If Sam got him to see that he needed to give it another chance, maybe Forrest would realize where he really belonged.

Sam raised a finger to his lips. If Charlee hadn't walked in, he'd have leaned all the way in.

The skin on Sam's finger still burned from touching Forrest's lips. It had been an automatic reaction; the deep-seated need to silence Forrest's self-deprecations.

But once he'd touched him... Sam swallowed as he looked at the lab work in front of him. A patient had an infection in a tooth.

The station's dentist, Dr. Abrams, had pulled the aching tooth, but that hadn't fixed the infection. And neither had the antibiotics Dr. Abrams had ordered.

Maybe Forrest has an idea?

Sam shook his head. There was no reason to ask Forrest. Not yet. Sam was in control of the clinic. This was why he'd been hired. He'd worked alone in so many places. He could figure it out, if his brain would focus on the numbers.

Or I could stop being ridiculous and ask the internal medicine doctor.

Sam's hand went for the phone on the desk. The headset was heavy in his hand. It might be nice to pretend that was because, before coming to the South Pole, he hadn't used a landline telephone for years. It wasn't like there was cell service here.

Now I'm thinking about a phone rather than calling the man who can take a look at this and figure it out.

"Any chance you have something for me to do?" Forrest asked the question as he was pushing the door of the clinic open. His lips were pursed. "I have three lab tests running. There's nothing to do for the next twelve hours. Staring at tubes is not very exciting."

Sam opened his mouth but didn't know what to say. It was like he'd conjured the man of his dreams.

At exactly the right time.

"Were you calling someone?" Forrest pointed to the phone in Sam's hand.

Sam finally registered the sound of the busy tone that meant the phone had been off the hook for too long.

"You. I was calling you." He set the phone back on the receiver. "Dr. Abrams pulled a tooth from one of the scientists two days ago. Raging infection in the jaw."

Forrest made a face. "I am glad dentists exist—I can't stand teeth. Something about them." He shuddered and rocked back on his heels, then raised his hands. "So no help with mouths."

"Actually, it's the bacteria I need help with. It's resistant to the antibiotic Dr. Abrams prescribed." Sam passed the tablet chart to Forrest. His arm vibrated as Forrest's thumb brushed his finger taking the chart.

Damn.

A simple touch was enough to light his entire body up.

"Bacteria?" Forrest looked over the notes on the chart.

"Yeah. And given our location and the limits of our stocks, Dr. Abrams wants to make sure the next one we give the patient isn't ignored by the bacteria, too. If this was a summer stint, the scientist would have been on a flight out to have oral surgery. But." Sam shrugged.

Everyone here knew the risks. If you came in the winter and had an emergency, there were no guarantees the weather would hold for you to be evacced. In fact, the odds were good no plane would arrive.

That did nothing to alleviate the pit in Sam's stomach. Every time you used an antibiotic against a resistant bacterium, there was a chance it created a superbug that was even more resistant.

"You have carbapenems?"

"Yeah. And tigecycline, doxycycline and a few doses of zosurabalpin." Sam had gone over their inventory of antibiotics used to treat resistant bacteria this morning. There were several, but it was still early in the season. If there were multiple patient needs—

He shut that thought down. No need to borrow worry.

Forrest looked at the tablet and closed his eyes, probably running through the mental storage cabinets in his brain. He didn't open his eyes as he started, "There is a good chance this a streptococcus oralis bacteria, given that it's the most prevalent cause of periodontal infections. According to a British study, twenty-seven percent of those are resistant to penicillin and amoxicillin. However, that study also found that only seven percent of the strains were resistant to clindamycin."

"I've got that. And the dental office has it, too." Sam picked up the phone, this time dialing the number with no hesitation. He relayed the information

Forrest had given to Dr. Abrams and set the phone down. "For someone who doesn't care about mouths and teeth, you pulled out a pretty specific statistic."

Color rushed to Forrest's cheeks as he passed the tablet back. Once again, their fingers brushed and the fire that hadn't died from last time exploded.

Sam's chest tightened, his heart cried out and his brain couldn't find any of the reasons he'd kept as a mantra for why he needed to keep his distance.

"I'm an internal medicine specialist who works in immunology. My reading list on antibiotics is deep. Not exactly light bedtime reading, but it comes in handy." Forrest pulled his lip between his teeth for a moment.

"No fiction? Sci-fi? Fantasy? I seem to remember you reading fantasy novels with witches, vampires, feys, back when we lived together." A smile touched Sam's lips as he said the last words.

Forrest looked toward the clinic door, but instead of heading for it, he took a step closer to the desk. "When I shifted out of the bedside to the lab, I put the fiction away."

He punished himself for making a change.

It was something his grandmother would have done. If you fail, then you lose something. The man needed to be back at bedside, needed to realize he *wasn't* a failure.

And there was no reason Sam couldn't find an excuse to have Forrest here in the clinic. He was good at planning. Good at sculpting life…as long as it wasn't his love life.

Sam stepped around the desk. "Forrest." He reached for his hands. There was no word to describe the rush of joy that poured through him when Forrest didn't pull away.

"You—"

The alarm on the wall echoed. Both men jumped back.

"What the hell is that?" Forrest looked at the red light as Sam picked up the phone on the first ring.

"Where?" Sam took the emergency information and set the phone back on the receiver.

Forrest was behind him as Sam took off running. "What are we running for?"

"We need bandages, wound care and anything else we have to treat burns. Fire suppression failed in the maintenance room. Two patients. One burned badly, the other unknown. I don't know what badly means." That would be Forrest's next question, so Sam was just going to answer it now.

It was a fair question, but one he hadn't had time to ask.

"We prepped for burn care?"

That answer to that was *It depends*. The station called the clinic the general hospital, but it wasn't a hospital by most people's definitions. "For second-degree superficial, yes. Full second-degree and third..." Sam swallowed the worry. There were a lot of *ifs* right now, but this was what he'd trained for. Emergency critical care. "We are a critical care unit, but I have no surgeons, no MRI or CT scanner.

If infection sets in or there is nerve damage... Well, we will cross that bridge if we get to it."

They gathered the materials, laid them out and then started for the front door. He'd waited for patients in the receiving bay a handful of times before, when he worked in trauma care in New York City. But it was an activity more reserved for television dramas than real life.

"If, Sam? Infection comes with burns. That's what burns do." Forrest spoke the truth as they headed for the front door.

With burns, crossing the bridge to infection was a near certainty. Second- and third-degree burns ripped away the protective layer of epidermis. And if they needed to do skin grafts, there were no supplies here.

The wind whipped Sam's face as he stared into the darkness. He'd wanted a reason for Forrest to be in the clinic. Now he had one. Sometimes it was best not to wish for anything.

"You can smell the smoke." Forrest stood next to him. "The ambulance isn't here yet. That isn't a good sign."

"I know." Sam bit out the words. His fingers tapped against the scrubs he was wearing. Neither of them had thrown on their coats. He'd expected to have sight of at least one of the two ambulances on their way to the clinic. Expected to stand outside for no more than a few moments.

"We have to go inside." Forrest grabbed Sam's arm, squeezing it. "Now."

Sam let Forrest pull him back in. He wanted to get

to the patients as soon as possible. With burn care, or any emergency care, time was of the essence. But if he and Forrest stood outside too long, frost bite was certain, and that wouldn't do their patients any good.

"Sam!" Natasha pushed through the front door. "You can smell the smoke, and I heard the alarm in my dorm room."

"Thanks for coming. Head into the clinic—get prepped for burn patients. We've already pulled supplies. I've got Forrest with me to meet the patients. When the critical patients get here, we need to be as ready as possible."

"Critical." Natasha's voice was low, but she rushed past them. "I'll call Chris."

"This is going to be a long night," Sam breathed out.

"It isn't just tonight. What are the odds of an evac?" Forrest's voice was low, too.

He knew the answer. Or at least had to suspect it. It was one thing to sign papers saying you understood the risk you were taking. Another to be face-to-face with the consequences.

"Almost zero. At least historically. I got Anderson out on the last flight for a reason. In previous winters, there have been exactly two evacs from McMurdo. The good news is that we aren't at Amundsen-Scott. The answer there is zero."

"Not zero is something we can work with," Forrest stated as they heard the ambulance pull up and stepped back outside.

"Doc!" Frank Opalin, the station's head paramedic,

was speaking as soon as he opened the door of the ambulance. "Mark's arm is bad. We loaded him first. But I got another on the way. That one isn't as bad but…" Frank pulled the stretcher out.

Mark's arm was elevated; his shirt had been cut away and wet bandages covered the arm. Tears were running down his face.

"I gave him pain meds." Frank held up the clipboard so Sam could see the exact amount. "Not that it's helping much."

That was actually a good sign. Not that Sam was going to waste time voicing it right now. If there was pain, it meant the nerves were still active. In the long run Mark would be happy about that. But it was little comfort now.

"I've got the next one." Forrest raised his chin. "See you in there."

Sam nodded and followed the gurney carrying Mark into the clinic.

CHAPTER SIX

"I KNOW IT hurts but we have to keep the arm elevated." Forrest made sure he kept his face devoid of emotion as he started redressing Mark's wound. Sam was on the other side of their patient, evaluating the burns Mark had sustained while pulling away from the fire.

The last four hours had been about stabilizing. But in order to keep the arm clean they were going to have change the dressings regularly, particularly because the wound was already seeping fluid through the bandages. Not the best sign, but not unexpected.

"I am going to up your morphine drip and give you a sedative." Sam said the words but Forrest wasn't sure Mark truly registered what he was saying. He'd told them not to sedate him when he came in. That he needed answers.

Informed consent was important, but with Mark in so much pain, Forrest knew the man wasn't able to focus on his care. The request to stay awake was just a sign of shock, of the fear that if you went to sleep something bad would happen.

It took a few minutes, but the sedative Sam placed in the IV took hold.

"The burns on his feet are superficial, thanks to his shoes, but the one on his side… It's deepening." Sam crossed his arms as he looked at Forrest.

"Deepening to superficial second-degree or into full partial thickness?" Most people didn't realize that burns could get worse over the course of hours or even days after the initial intake. Particularly when they were more than superficial.

"I am hoping we can keep it at superficial." Sam took a deep breath.

"*We* can't do anything but wait." Forrest waited for Sam to meet his gaze. It took a minute, but Sam finally met his eyes. "The burns will be what they will be. We can keep him comfortable and do our best to prevent infection. The rest is out of our hands right now."

There was nothing to do but wait and worry. This scenario. This dread and uncertainty. This was the reason Forrest had failed at bedside.

Sam nodded, but the twitch in his cheek meant the message hadn't been well received. Sam was a doctor dedicated to getting his patients the best care. It was admirable, but there were some things no doctor could fix. Sam needed to focus on what they could control, not what he wanted to control.

"His arm…" Sam didn't finish the sentence. But there wasn't any need.

Forrest understood. The side was bad, and maybe getting worse. With the arm, they already knew the worst was here.

Mark needed at least one skin graft by the elbow. It was possible his forearm was going to need one, too. Luckily his fingers were surface burns, sustained when he'd pushed the blazing equipment off his arm. A small miracle that was hard to focus on when there was no way they could offer the necessary procedures here. And the storm that had set in just after they'd gotten Mark and his fellow mechanic Adina into the clinic meant the odds of an evac in the next forty-eight hours was zero. And probably not much better than that for at least the next week.

"Right now we focus on pain reduction and infection control." Forrest kept his repeated words quiet. Sam falling into what-ifs and worries wasn't going to help the patient.

Plus, Adina was in the other bay. She would be listening in, hoping to hear what was happening with her friend. The pair had partnered at the south pole for two summer seasons. This was their first winter over.

"Is he going to be okay?" The call came over the curtain.

Sam looked at the curtain and frowned. "I can't tell you anything, Adina. It's protocol."

"Protocol my ass!" Adina was shifting in her bed.

Forrest started toward the other bay and knew Sam was following him. He rounded the corner and hoped his smile looked comforting and not panicked.

She wasn't going to like the words Sam was delivering. "Adina, we can't give patient care out to non-family members."

"We are family." The woman crossed her arms and let out a hiss as she rubbed the burns on her fingers. Luckily, her wounds were mostly superficial. There was one they were watching, a burn on her shin from an ember catching on her pants while she pulled Mark to safety. Though it wasn't second-degree, it was close. But she didn't need a skin graft. Her recovery was going to be rough, but a hell of a lot easier than Mark's.

She pointed to the bay where Mark was in the medicinally induced nap. "Family does not mean dating. It does not mean married or screwing." She sucked in a deep breath. "We are friends. Best friends. His wife divorced him a year ago and I have no interest in a relationship. We're neighbors back home, run a mechanics training business when we aren't here."

"I understand, Adina." Forrest said the words before Sam could. Because from him, they were the truth.

Sam had a family that loved him. Something Forrest was so grateful for.

But Forrest had no family. His grandmother was meeting whatever fate waited in the afterlife. He had no idea who his father was and no interest in taking any commercial DNA tests to possibly find out. His mother had bounced in and out of jail for most of his life for petty and not so petty financial crimes. Last he'd heard she was serving twenty for the latest insurance fraud she'd run.

Sam had been his family long before they were dating. And rekindling their friendship had wiped away so much of the loneliness that had been his only companion for years.

A tear slipped down Adina's cheek. "I am his family. So tell me, please."

Forrest's heart squeezed as Sam swallowed.

"I am bound by HIPAA here. I can't give you details." Sam's jeweled gaze met his.

Forrest weighed the risk and stepped around Sam. If it cost him, it cost him. "He needs a procedure we can't do here."

He felt Sam tense beside him, but he didn't say anything.

"A skin graft." Adina nodded. "I know burns, man. You don't work in heavy machinery and mechanics without seeing injuries." She closed her eyes and shook as tears streamed down her cheeks. "The weather means evac is impossible for at least a week."

"It might not be a week," Sam interrupted and was rewarded with a glare when Adina opened her eyes.

"You're right. It's probably a lot longer than that."

Sam lowered his head. There were no comforting words rushing into Forrest's mind to help the situation. Sam couldn't control the weather. No amount of planning would magically make an evac appear when the visibility and wind made any flight so dangerous.

"Do you want a sedative? With the burns and the worry I doubt you'll get much sleep, and your body needs it for healing." Sam took a step toward the medicine cabinet as the silence stretched between them all.

Forrest wanted to push. Wanted to urge Adina to accept the sedation. Sam was right; it would help her recover. Her burns were not as substantial as Mark's, but her body still had a lot of repair to accomplish. But in his experience combative patients did not appreciate the push.

"Why, so you can discuss his procedures and needs without me hearing?" And Adina was hostile. Hostile on behalf of her friend, but still hostile.

"I know you're mad about the requirements that are legally in place. When Mark wakes, we can ask him to sign documentation agreeing to have you as a care partner. That's all I can offer right now, but I understand your reaction." Sam moved next to the bed, medication in his hand.

"Do you? Do you have a friend that, if they were hurt, you'd want to know everything? *Need* to do everything to make sure that they were okay. That you would run through fire for...literally." Adina glared at the medication then back at Sam.

"Yes." Sam answered with no hesitation. "I have someone who is incredibly special to me. Who would make me feel exactly the way you do. I understand the anger and frustration." Sam took a deep breath as he kept his gaze on Adina.

"Take the medication, Adina. Get the rest. Fight for Mark tomorrow." Forrest heard himself say the words, but it was like he was watching a movie, not participating in the event. He was outside looking in.

He tried to stop the buzzing in his ears. Tried to shut off the feeling ripping through him. Sam had said he'd kept to himself since his engagement ended. That he had no friends. That he was a lone wolf now. Forrest had had to force him into this friendship.

But there was someone. Someone special to him. Someone he hadn't told Forrest about. Someone he'd kept hidden.

They were exes. He could hardly demand full entry into Sam's life. The jealousy in the pit of his stomach was unfair. He should be happy. Joyful even. Sam hadn't cut himself completely out of people's lives.

But all he wanted to do was scream. Demand to know why he'd said there was no one.

Instead, Forrest looked at Adina, holding her gaze. "Take it."

Her glare didn't let up, but she did nod and look at Sam. "Fine. But I will make sure that Mark tells you both that we are family and signs whatever you need, because he is going to need an advocate here."

"I know you will." Sam pushed the meds into her system and after a few minutes she was yawning and slipping into slumber.

Forrest moved toward the door. "I think my skills aren't needed right now. We should save our strength for the rotation we're going to need to maintain for Mark and Adina's care. Give me a ring if anything changes." He needed to leave. Needed to gather himself. A few minutes to handle the passion he'd heard in Sam's voice as he spoke about this unknown friend.

A few minutes to push past the wish that it was him.

"Wait!" Sam held up his hand as Forrest was heading for the door. The outburst was unplanned, but he also didn't want him to leave.

He'd meant what he said to Adina. If something

happened to Forrest, despite the distance, the time, all of life between them, he'd need to know.

"What?" Forrest tilted his head as he leaned against the door.

The man had no right to look so enticing after such a long shift. His dark hair was rumpled and there were shadows under his eyes, but he was still so lovely to gaze at.

"I meant it, you know." Sam bit his lip to stop everything else from bursting forth.

"Meant what?" Forrest never moved from the doorway. Never adjusted his position.

"Come on, Forrest." Sam blew out a breath. "I said it once and I said it with passion and honestly, I don't remember all the words at the moment. But come *on*."

Forrest's face shifted, those dark eyes capturing Sam's own. The uncertainty Sam saw there nearly destroyed him. How could Forrest never think he was enough? Never consider that good words were about him?

"I really don't know what you mean, Sam. It's been a long day."

"If it was me in that bed and you in Adina's position, would you need to know?" Sam took a deep breath then kept going, "Would you fight to get an answer? Even if it wasn't a full one. Enough to know what was happening?"

"Yes." Now Forrest shifted, but didn't close any distance. "If it was you, I would need to know. I probably wouldn't have sat in the bed. I would have been in the way, being the reason every physician hates having family members with medical backgrounds in the room. Why?"

"You are so dense. So damn dense." Sam moved. If Forrest wouldn't leave the doorway, then Sam would go to him. "*You* are the person I was telling Adina about. You are the one that I need to know is safe." He balled his fists wanting to beat them against Forrest's chest—to punch each line into his heart.

"I… I figured it was someone you met after we parted."

"We didn't part." Sam shook his head. "*You* broke my heart and walked away." He sucked air into his lungs. This wasn't the place. Wasn't the time. Wasn't anything. But damn, getting the words out released a bubble of tension he hadn't known his soul had kept a hold of so long.

"Sam—"

"No. I don't need words from you, right now. I just need you to finally understand why being your friend is so damn hard. But also impossible to give up." He stepped back, "Also you were great at bedside today. I know you feel like you failed there before, but the doctor you were tonight was perfection. *You* were perfect."

Work. An easy topic. A necessary one. And one that could put distance between them. That was safeish. That might keep all the emotions he'd trapped so long ago from spilling out of his chest.

"Tonight was awful," he went on, "but there is no one I would rather have stood with tonight. Even if you did kinda give out information about a patient you shouldn't have." He winked, hoping this would diffuse the rumbling feelings still trying to burst their way through.

Forrest pursed his lips and looked toward the bays where Mark and Adina slept. "Technically, all I said was he needed a procedure we couldn't do here. She guessed. And we didn't give details. It's not technically a HIPAA violation."

"It skirts the rules." Sam looked to the bays. "I seem to remember that was something you did more than once at bedside. Found ways to make sure people got care even after insurance or a hospital administrator said no."

Most of the interns had followed every protocol human resources demanded. Not wanting to step out of place, even a hair. Even Sam.

Sam was willing to go out on a limb, occasionally. When he knew winning was a certainty. But Forrest had taken risks. Even knowing it might cost him residency recommendations.

"I was always able to rise to an emergency situation. Doesn't mean I can do it full-time." Forrest made to cross his arms but didn't. He rolled on his heels but didn't head out of the door.

Now Sam did put his fist to Forrest's chest, ignoring the lightning bolts traipsing up his arm with each touch as he punctuated his thoughts. "Stop selling yourself short, Forrest. Just stop."

Forrest's hand was warm as he gripped Sam's fist. "Take a breath."

"Not until you admit that you are damn good at

this." Sam didn't pull away from Forrest's touch. And he didn't drop his hand.

"Planning to hold your breath to make your point?" Forrest raised an eyebrow. If they weren't in the clinic and reacting to a night full of emotions, Sam might just lean in and kiss the handsome man standing opposite him.

"Maybe that's exactly what I will do." Sam inhaled but couldn't stop the chuckles as Forrest bent over and let out a belly laugh, too.

The laughter carried. It was a good thing both their patients were on sedatives.

"You two losing it?" Chris stomped in, hanging his coat on the hanger and stripping off his heavy snow boots and sliding on the tennis shoes he kept at the clinic.

"Maybe." Forrest stepped away from Sam's touch.

Sam watched him flex his hand. Watched him put it in his pocket and turn to Chris. Had the connection felt as fiery to him?

"It was a long night. The first of many, I suspect." Forrest looked over his shoulder at the bay. "I'll be part of the rotation for as long as they're here."

"Starting to feel like you're a real part of the team." Chris hit Forrest on the shoulder.

Sam looked at Forrest and nodded. He was part of the team. An important part of it. He was grateful someone else was pointing it out.

"Fill me on the patients then you head out too, Doc. 'Cause I expect to have you and Natasha here relieving me first thing tomorrow." Chris pointed toward

Forrest. "Of course if you're on the rotation, then we can run two shifts of full staff. Actually, that's a good idea, I'm calling Nat. I know she works night shift at home anyway. You two pop in here tomorrow on time."

"Did we just get orders from the NP?" Forrest raised a brow.

"Yep. And if you know many NPs, then you know not to argue." Chris crossed his arms.

Forrest held up his hands. "No plan to argue. And I meant what I said. I'll see you tomorrow." He looked to Sam. "Good night, Sam."

The cool burst of air the snow doors didn't capture hit Sam, and the ember of hope that Forrest might hang out long enough for him to debrief Chris flamed out.

CHAPTER SEVEN

MARK'S ARM LOOKED bad the next morning. That wasn't a surprise. But at least it didn't look as bad as Sam had feared it might. The skin sloughing was expected.

"You gonna tell me how bad it is?" Mark crossed his good hand over his stomach. "I mean the drugs are keeping the edge off, but I know I need a skin graft."

"Adina tell you?" Sam had wanted to broach that topic himself. Let Mark ask any questions he might have and hopefully control any worry the man would understandably have about the situation. But Mark had signed the paperwork granting his friend access as soon he'd woken and she'd already known.

"No. She is lying to me. Says I'm fine."

"I heard that," Adina called over the curtain.

"I meant you to," Mark yelled back, though his voice wasn't as solid as Adina's.

Sam looked to the door. Forrest had grabbed a few samples from Mark's arm first thing to look for infection. Normally they'd wait until they got the first signs of it but given the need for an evac that wasn't coming, they were going to be checking several times a day.

Evac wasn't coming this week and probably not next week, either. If they pretreated with antibiotics, there was a worry that the bacteria would adjust and they'd run out of treatment options before an evac was possible. So they were doing everything they could to stay ahead of it. With any luck they could prevent it or catch it in its infancy.

"Come on, Doc. Tell the truth." Mark's eyes filled with tears but they didn't fall as he lifted his chin.

This was what Forrest struggled with. This was the part of bedside work that everyone hated. But it was necessary.

"You need at least two skin grafts on your arm. And maybe one on your thigh from where you were dragged across the room."

"You hear that, Adina? You did such a piss-poor job of dragging me that I need a patch on my thigh. You're going to owe me beers for life." Mark chuckled but he brushed the lone tear sliding down his cheek away.

"Nah," Adina called out. "You panicked when you caught fire. If you hadn't wussed out then maybe it wouldn't be so bad. I owe you beer for a year. Tops."

"Two years."

At least Adina's jabs were keeping Mark's mood up. Or as up as it could be in the circumstances.

Forrest walked in and marched over to the bay. Then he pushed the curtain back so the two patients had a full view of each other. "I can hear you two yelling before I even get close to the building."

There was no way that was true with the wind. But Sam suspected you could hear them as soon as the outer door opened.

"Just trying to be normal since someone got themself burned to a crisp." Adina glared at her friend. Sam wasn't sure if it was meant to be playful or not.

"Took them long enough to open the curtain." Mark rolled his eyes before looking at Forrest. "What's the outcome, Doc Two?"

"Doc Two?" Forrest looked up from the clipboard he was carrying with the results. It was old-school but with the weather right now the internet was even worse than usual.

Sam let out a relieved sigh and saw Mark's eyes flick to him.

"You annoyed that Doc Two is avoiding my answer?"

"Nope. If Doc Two, as you call him, is asking a question not related to care, then that workup came back as clean as possible." Sam grinned. It was one of Forrest's tells when they were in med school. If the prognosis was good, he was willing to entertain a little diversion. If not…

Well, if not, the man was all business.

Forrest blew out a breath. "Your labs—"

"I called you Doc Two because this guy—" Mark pointed at Sam as he interrupted Forrest "—is Doc. I can't say Doc to you as well, so you are Doc Two."

"All right." Forrest's brows knitted together. "Your labs."

"I think my jokes are fab."

"They aren't." Adina laughed.

Mark shifted in the bed and winced. He was on enough pain medication to be as comfortable as possible. But there was no way for them to keep him lucid without some residual pain. "I know the results are good. Because Doc seems to know you well. And I'm only going to get good news on rare occasions. I need to savor the moment." Mark pinched his eyes shut. "Damn it, there's no reason for tears."

"Tears provide a release to your parasympathetic nervous system. Your body uses it to self-soothe and regulate your emotions." Forrest stepped closer to the bed. "You're correct. This lab is good. It shows the wet bandages are keeping the infection at bay. I may not be able to say the same thing tomorrow, or even this afternoon. But, putting off good news to savor it is normal. And crying is normal."

"Has the home base started recommending removing the arm, since evac may be weeks away?" Mark sucked in a breath as he looked at Forrest, dread clear in his eyes.

Forrest looked to Sam. This was an answer he couldn't give. Technically Forrest was on staff here, but this was not his full-time position.

"We are way off from that discussion." They weren't. And Mark was right. His bosses back in Houston had given the advice that they may need to amputate. Their email indicated they were already thinking of it as an inevitability.

Amputation was risky, too. If it came to it, Sam would be able to follow his field training but he was not a general surgeon. Years ago, an orthopedic surgeon had used the remote telemedicine connection to coach a doctor at Amundsen-Scott through repairing a knee. The Center for Polar Medical Operations was already looking for a specialist to do the same for Sam. But it wasn't going to come to that.

It wasn't. He wouldn't allow it. He and Forrest could keep the arm infection-free and the weather would break. It had to.

He saw Forrest's head shift toward him out of the corner of his eye but didn't look in his direction.

Mark took a deep breath and closed his eyes. "That's good to hear. Two pieces of good news. Good day." He closed his eyes. "I'm going to try to take a nap. Okay?"

"Sure," Sam stated.

"Absolutely," Forrest answered at the same time.

"I was talking to the mouthy woman in the bay next to me, Doc and Doc Two. Appreciate the support, though." Mark gave a thumbs up with his good hand and closed his eyes.

"If you can't sleep, I can provide another sedative." The best thing for Mark was for his body to rest. However, that was easier said than done when the body could only focus on pain—even pain curbed by the drugs in his system.

Mark didn't open his eyes, but he shook his head. "I'm gonna try and do this without those, at least for a nap."

Sam nodded even though Mark couldn't see him. Then he stepped around the bed, stepped into the bay next to Mark and closed the curtain.

"You don't have to worry. I won't try to keep him awake." Adina blew out a breath as she looked at the curtain separating them.

Forrest stepped in and offered a smile. "We know that, Adina. But we need to discuss your care."

Sam saw Forrest look over the tablet chart. He'd taken responsibility for her care, so it was his job to do the discharge.

"You're going to be sore for a few days. But the good news is the burn we were worried about didn't deepen."

"So I don't need an evac?" Adina looked at the closed curtain.

Forrest shook his head, "No. I'm going to give you antibiotics. It's very important that you take them. Your recovery should be fairly easy, at least compared to Mark's."

"Which is your way of saying get out." Adina sat up and looked over to where Mark was trying to sleep.

"You can come back anytime." Forrest didn't look at Sam as he bluntly spoke against the actual clinic policy. "I know we have visiting hours and everything, but we will make an exception for you to check on Mark."

No hesitation. No worry that Sam might balk. Of course he wouldn't. Mark needed to know that he could have company anytime. It was good for his soul.

But even if Sam hadn't been willing to break the rules, Forrest would have found a way.

"Doc all right with that?" Adina focused her gaze on Sam as she waited for confirmation.

"I am."

She pushed a tear from her cheek. "It isn't that I don't trust you."

Forrest nodded. "Of course. You just need to see for yourself."

"My brother..." She hiccupped, "My parents accepted everything the doctor said. Didn't question the discharge. Didn't point out that he was so good at hiding pain because of his chronic issues. And..." Adina stopped and looked back at Forrest, "I will be Mark's advocate. You will be so sick of seeing me."

"I look forward to you keeping us on our toes. An extra set of eyes that knows him better than we ever will is appreciated." Sam understood what had happened with her brother without her completing the sentence.

He also understood how it could happen. Hospitals were busy places. In the US, many hospitals were run by private equity firms that prioritized profits over patients. When you combined that with insurance companies demanding tons of paperwork to justify every extra night in a hospital, it was far too easy for a patient who was good at masking symptoms to slip through the cracks.

Hell, it was easy for a patient who was manifesting their symptoms as loudly as possible to slip through the cracks.

"I think you actually mean that." She took the tablet from Forrest, and signed the electronic forms then slid off the bed and grabbed her things.

"You will be on quarters for at least the rest of the week. No working until those fingers are fully healed. And you *need* to take your antibiotics. That burn on your leg is deep enough that if it gets infected there could be problems." Forrest passed Sam the tablet.

"Right, Doc Two. Take meds. Don't get infection." She rolled her eyes.

"I don't need two evac patients." Sam winked at Adina as she and Forrest walked past him to head out.

Forrest was back in moments, standing opposite the desk where Sam had retreated to put the notes about Mark into the clinical record. Forrest put both hands on the desk and leaned over it.

It would have been sexy as hell, if his eyes weren't smoldering in a furious, not fun, way.

"We need to talk."

"We *are* at the point of discussing amputation." Forrest made sure he kept his voice very low. Mark was snoring, but there was no guarantee the man wouldn't wake at any instant. And he wanted to make sure that when this conversation came up—and it was going to come up—that Mark heard it in a kind and gentle way, not from overhearing his doctors arguing.

"It's not." Sam leaned back in his chair. Was he pulling away from him, or uncomfortable with the confrontation over patient care?

Probably both.

Forrest stood and drew a hand over his face. "I know that Houston has already told you they're examining all the options, Sam."

Sam flinched at the soft way he said his name. Forrest didn't want to argue. Didn't want any distance between them. But this was important.

"They are. But the weather is going to break and we are going to make sure he stays infection-free." Sam's clipped words struck against Forrest's soul.

There was no way for them to promise any of those things. So much of this was out of their control. This was why he'd failed at bedside, because reality was a hard master.

"You can't plan your way through this, Sam."

"Don't *Sam* me. Don't." Sam leaned forward, dark circles under his eyes highlighted against his sunken skin.

Forrest started again, "The road we are on is treacherous. There are no guarantees."

"I know that." Sam pushed out of the chair and put his hands on the desk like Forrest had done a few minutes ago. "I know there are no guarantees. But this is something we can and will control."

Forrest looked at his feet, took a deep breath and carefully chose his words. "How are you planning to control the weather?" When he looked up, he wasn't surprised by the steel in Sam's gaze.

Sam always had a plan. A goal. A place he was moving toward. But he needed to understand the control he'd always tried to maintain over his life wasn't possible. At least not here. They needed to be ready for an evac…and a worst-case scenario.

Sam opened his mouth then snapped it shut.

"And infection? Have you found a way to ensure

no germs get into the wound? Because if so, you will win the Nobel in medicine. There won't even be a competition for it."

"Stop making fun of me." Sam pinched his eyes close.

"I'm not. But I apologize if my words could be misinterpreted. That means I was far from clear." Forrest waited a moment but Sam didn't say anything so he continued, "Perfection isn't possible here."

"I left my perfectionism gene behind long ago." Now his stormy gaze met Forrest's. "I know life isn't fair. I know what Houston is saying. I know what the damn weather forecast looks like. But I am going to find a way to control this outcome."

Forrest reached his hand across the desk, gently laying his hand on Sam's. He didn't pull away and Forrest's soul sighed at the connection. But it was comfort he was offering, not anything else.

"You are a perfectionist—it's part of you. One doesn't just lose the thing that pushed them to be their best. It's what led to your high grades in med school."

"Not as high as yours." Sam stuck out his tongue but still didn't pull away.

"It's what led you to push yourself so hard on crew. You rowed at four a.m. while listening to lectures on headphones while others were listening to rock music to keep their speed up." It was one of the grumbles Forrest had voiced more than once. They never got to sleep in because Sam was out the door long before the sun rose.

"There wasn't anyone else there, Forrest. It was just me, my study guide and the ergometer." Sam's thumb ran along Forrest's thumb.

Forrest didn't look down at the connection. If he did, he'd lose his train of thought and this was important.

"This conversation is not about the rowing machine. You can't follow a carefully laid plan to get the exact result you want here. You can't promise things." Forrest expected his own words to bring up a need to return to the lab. To seal himself away with his microscopes and slides that couldn't feel hurt. But the feeling didn't come.

It was a weird sensation. He was facing up to the possibility of delivering bad news, and yet he wasn't aching to get out. Wasn't wondering whether it was clear to everybody that he felt like a fake. For the first time in forever, he felt at home in a clinic.

"I know I can't," Sam said. "And I know that we might have to do something I have never done and have no desire to do." He swallowed and still didn't pull his hand from Forrest's.

Forrest should retreat. Pull back. Put the distance they'd sworn to keep back in place.

Who was he kidding? They'd broken that rule nearly as soon as they'd announced it.

"But Mark can have another day of good news," Sam went on. "Another moment to keep hope. And so can I. Because I know Amundsen-Scott did the knee surgery via telemedicine, but this is not knee surgery. This is…"

Forrest squeezed Sam's hand. "If it comes to it, I'll be by your side."

"I don't want it to come to that."

"Neither do I." Forrest squeezed his fingers one more time, then he lifted his hand, ignoring the soft cry from his heart that it wasn't ready to let go. It would never be ready.

Sam picked his hand up, rubbing his palms together. The two stared at each other for a moment. What were they supposed to say now?

"I heard from my parents yesterday. I meant to tell you they say hi." Sam smiled.

Words said so loosely. So easily.

"I assumed they hated me." Forrest hadn't meant to speak those words. Ed and Georgina, who everyone called Georgie, were the sweetest people. They'd welcomed him into their home. Sent a birthday gift and made sure he had presents under the tree from someone besides their son.

When he'd had a win at school or as an intern, he could call them and tell them like they were his parents, too. The day he'd walked away from bedside he nearly dialed their number. He'd even pulled it up in his phone, aching for someone to hear his worry. To tell him the path he was choosing was the right one.

"I don't think they know how to hate," Sam said. "I mean, they were shocked and hurt for me, but they missed you, too." He stretched his arms over his head and his shoulder popped.

"You're getting creaky." Forrest chuckled as the smile spread across Sam's face.

"I am. I think it was all that time spent on the erg." He looked at the door then back at Forrest. "I need to put notes in. Mark is sleeping. You can go back to your lab for a while. If I need you, I'll call."

Forrest wrapped his arms around himself and tried to find any reason he might need to hang around. But nothing came. Sam had dismissed him. And there was no point in staying.

CHAPTER EIGHT

Sam pulled at the erg handle, relishing the burn the rowing machine gave his muscles. He'd been up since three and given up on the idea of finding sleep again sometime after four.

It would be nice to blame the South Pole for the insomnia. After all, it was a common complaint at the pole's research centers. But it wasn't a messed-up circadian rhythm keeping Sam from rest.

Forrest.

The man's face danced across Sam's tired mind and he pulled harder on the bar. His split time was going to be amazing but the workout wasn't accomplishing the goal of driving Forrest from his mind.

Forrest.

He'd dreamed of him for the last three nights. Each night the dream lasting a little longer. Last night Sam had kissed him. Held him. Clung to him.

After they'd separated, Sam had dreamed of Forrest every night for a year, his subconscious torturing him with good memories. With feelings he was never going to get again.

He'd woken this morning with the feel of Forrest's lips still on his. The scent of him whispering through the dream. If Sam put his fingers to his lips, he might feel the ghost of him even now.

He yanked harder on the erg to keep his fingers from following through on the thought.

"You're up early. No one's ever in here when I

come this early." Forrest's chin was covered with stubble and he looked so damn good in that tight gray T-shirt and loose black shorts.

It was almost as if Sam's thoughts had conjured him. Like he was still dreaming.

"Couldn't sleep." He pulled on the handle and flinched at the burn running down his shoulders. *Relax.*

He'd rowed for years. He knew the form he needed and knew the risk of injury if he didn't follow it. Didn't mean it was easy for his body to slide back into it as Forrest stretched beside the treadmill.

"Thinking about Mark?" Forrest pulled an arm across his center then bent over to stretch his hips and legs.

Sam made sure to keep his eyes focused on the wall in front of him. The last thing his subconscious needed was updates added to the memory jar for his dreams.

"No. I wasn't thinking of Mark." The words slipped out and he wanted to slap himself. That was the easy answer. The right answer. The answer that would drive the line of questions away.

Thinking about a burn patient was a good reason to be awake at this hour. Dreaming, fantasizing really, about your ex was very much not. Particularly when that ex was the one asking the question.

"Why can't you sleep then?" Forrest stepped onto the treadmill and pushed the button to start a slow jog.

Sam had cheered him on through six marathons

and more half marathons than he could count. He'd always made sure he was at the finish line with a sign and kiss. "You still run marathons?"

It wasn't an answer to Forrest's question but Forrest didn't say anything about that as he shook his head no.

"I stick to halves and 10Ks these days. Less training time." He wasn't even breathing hard as he pushed the treadmill speed up.

"Oh, yeah." Sam kept his tone light. "Thirteen miles and six miles are no distance at all."

"A little over six point two miles technically." Forrest stuck out his tongue as he upped the speed on the treadmill again.

"A little over six point two." Sam rolled his eyes and pulled on the handle of the erg as he repeated Forrest's words.

"No need to pick on me." Forrest chuckled and he pushed the speed up more. "How long have you been on that machine?" He adjusted the elevation and finally started breaking a sweat.

His gaze met Sam's as his feet pounded on the tread. If Sam was running and looked around like that, he'd trip over his feet and face plant.

"Don't avoid *this* question. How long, Sam?"

"I don't know. Over an hour." Sam stuck his tongue out, mirroring Forrest's earlier move.

"An hour on an erg? You do realize you aren't training for the Olympics anymore, right?" Forrest blew out a heavy breath as his feet continued to pound the treadmill. "Or are you training again?"

"No, I'm not training again. Those days are behind me." A ridiculous question added to point out the obvious. He'd worked out for far longer while aiming to make the Olympic team. But it wasn't necessary anymore. That didn't mean he was going to stop rowing. He usually stuck to forty-five minutes. But he was not stopping now, at least not until Forrest stopped running. Purely on principle.

"How long are you running?"

"How long are you rowing?" Forrest raised a brow before turning his attention to the stats on his machine.

"Not stopping until you do." It was silly. Playful, even though Sam's muscles were burning and his split pace had slowed considerably. A rowing machine was a full-body exercise and he'd not done more than an hour in years. He'd feel it tomorrow. But hopefully he'd get a night of dreamless rest.

Forrest chuckled and pressed the button to speed up the machine again.

He ran and Sam rowed in silence for the next several minutes. He could almost pretend they were just two men who happened to be in the gym at the same time rather than former lovers thrust back into each other's lives.

"Five miles. Done." Forrest panted as he hit the stop button and kept time as the treadmill slowed down.

"How the hell did you get five miles? You basically just started." Sam let go of the handle grateful to see it pop back into the rowing machine. Then he stood, ignoring the burn in his back and legs.

Forrest blew out a breath as he stretched by the machine. "It's a light day so I only do five. I run a little over a five-minute mile so done in thirty."

"Well, nice workout." Sam nodded and started for the door.

"Wait."

His stomach tightened and lightning shot through his body. Sam turned, focusing on keeping all of his emotions in check. "What?"

Color was cresting along Forrest's cheeks but he didn't break Sam's gaze. "You were on that machine for well over an hour and a half. If you don't stretch your body is going to tense up and you'll be sore for days."

He was going to be sore anyway. "I'll stretch in my room."

"No." Forrest shook his head. "To get to your room you have to go outside. The cold will tighten you up. Stretch here. I will stay quiet, but you are not hurting yourself just because you don't want to be around me."

"Don't want to be around you?" Sam took a step forward. "Hell, I am here *because* of you. I can't sleep because of you. I dream of you. My thoughts wander to you in every single free moment of the day and even some of the times when I'm supposed to be accomplishing something. *You*—" Sam pushed his finger into Forrest's chest "—are the only person I want to be around."

Suddenly, Forrest's lips were on his. His strong arms wrapped around him and the world tilted back into the right position for the first time in years. Sam leaned into him. Grasping Forrest's body as their tongues entwined and years of separation vanished.

Forrest was home and peace. The past and the present.

His fingers splayed across Sam's back, and Sam ran his hands through Forrest's dark hair, craving the feel of him after so many dreams.

Sam's hand moved from Forrest's hair to his face, running a thumb over the stubble on his cheeks before finally pulling back.

Both men stared at each other and the silence seemed to drag on infinitely longer than the kiss.

"That was not stretching—technically." Forrest bit his lip as he let out a soft chuckle. "Bad joke. Sorry."

"Don't apologize." Sam could stand a lot of things in this life but not Forrest apologizing for kissing him.

"I was saying sorry for the bad joke. The awkwardness I created after." Forrest pulled one arm behind his back. "Not the kiss. I..."

Whatever he'd planned to say after that fell away.

"It was quite the kiss." Sam barely caught his hand from lifting to run his fingers over his lips. His mind was going to have a field day filling in his dreams from now on.

"It was." Forrest pursed his lips and looked at the door. "If you don't want to stretch, I won't make you.

But don't come crying to me when your body is so sore you can barely move."

Sam shrugged. He needed to get going and he'd stretch in his room quickly before he hopped in the shower. "I have to get to the clinic. I'll have the samples ready for you to test as soon as you get there."

He turned toward the door, then turned back. "I'm glad you interrupted my workout."

Forrest shook his head. "I'm in here every day at the same time." He pointed a finger toward Sam but didn't step closer. "*You* interrupted my workout. And I am glad you did."

The hot shower had done nothing to drive his thoughts away from Sam. Forrest put on his coat, pulled the beanie over his still damp hair and looked at the door. He needed to head to the clinic and pick up the samples.

But that meant facing the aftermath of the kiss. It had happened without him thinking. A reaction based entirely on emotion, something Forrest tried very hard to avoid. After all, he'd spent his entire childhood paying for the sins of his mother's inability to control herself.

Forrest prided himself on his control. His ability to step back when the emotions got heated. But when Sam's fingertip dug into his chest all rational thought had vanished.

Running a finger over his lip, Forrest closed his eyes re-creating the moment in his mind. Sam was perfection. His kisses still curled Forrest's toes and sent his soul to the moon.

For a moment, a not so brief moment, everything seemed right in the universe. Like nature was sighing in relief that the two of them were connected.

"Stop being ridiculous." Forrest shook his head. The universe did not care about him. And if it was really watching, it wanted something more for Sam.

He's not taking more.

Forrest pinched his eyes closed. He'd worked with his therapist; he knew that wasn't a safe thought. Wasn't an accurate thought.

Still feels that way, though.

Nope. He was shutting this down. They'd kissed. Then Sam had said he had to go to the clinic and Forrest had let him go.

It was a good memory to add to his bank but didn't have to mean anything else.

Who am I trying to fool?

His mind wasn't going to accept any answer there so Forrest pulled the door open and marched his way through the cold and snow to the clinic building. At least the chill finally cooled the blood the kiss had ignited.

"I have the samples." Sam was at his side before he even had a chance to take off his coat. "There's infection developing. The arm is warm to the touch and he has a low-grade fever. I need these typed as soon as possible. I am doing everything I can today to get an evac out. It has to be now." The container holding the sample slides was pushed into Forrest's hands. "Please hurry."

Forrest nodded and headed back out into the snow. This wasn't the worst-case scenario. Low grade fever and warm were simply the start of an infection. But it wasn't good, either.

The fact that they'd kept infection at bay for almost two weeks was no small accomplishment. But that accomplishment meant nothing if they ended up having to perform the amputation. A risk that rose with every passing hour, let alone day.

Forrest forced his way back through the wind and ice toward his lab. The odds of an evac were still close to zero. The storm had broken last night and the wind was less intense, but that didn't mean help was coming.

If we don't get the infection under control...

Forrest shut that thought off, too. No use catastrophizing. A term his therapist had had him use to identify the thoughts that did not help him.

He got the samples under the microscope and saw what looked like bacterial growth. He'd start the bacterial enzyme test, leave a note for Charlee to call as soon as the test was done. With any luck it would take closer to four hours to have an answer, rather than twenty-four. But until the test completed there was no way to be sure.

The wind felt like it had died down as he headed back to the clinic. Or maybe that was just him wishing for a change so an evac might happen.

He pushed open the door and wasn't surprised when Sam strode through the inner door.

"I don't have news other than it looks bacterial, which isn't surprising." Forrest took his coat off and hung it on the peg. "I left a note for Charlee to call when the enzyme test completes. Is Mark resting?"

"Yes." Sam blew out a breath. "I talked to Houston and they say they might have an evac option open late tonight. The weather looks like it might hold. It's a strong might."

Sam had said the word *might* three times. Trying to remind himself, or to force it into being by pure force of will?

So the wind really had died down then. Now they just needed it to hold.

Adina burst through the door and Forrest let out a yelp as the blast of cold air hit his now–coat-free body.

"Don't stand in here, if you don't want to get cold." Adina barked as she took off her coat and walked past them. "Weather is breaking."

"How do you know?" Sam asked as he followed her.

Forrest took up the rear.

"I've done multiple stints here. Snowstorms happen in the summer too. You get a feel for it. The money is good and you get a feel for things. You need to call whoever it is and get a plane here. Now." She pointed her finger at Sam.

Adina's face was stern, but the wobble in her lip gave away the fear. "And you need to tell them the evac is for two." She lifted her pants, showing off the burn she'd received. It was swollen and angry.

Dark red lines grew from it. It looked like the infection was traveling. Lymphangitis or cellulitis symptoms. Both critical.

They'd spent so much time worrying over Mark they'd never even considered this. Adina had been here every day. And always said she was fine. Never let Forrest see it, though. And he hadn't pushed. She should have healed as long as she took the antibiotics.

The truth hit him as he looked at the red streaks and drainage.

"You aren't taking the antibiotics we gave you." Forrest kept his tone level, not accusing just observing.

Sam's eyes widened but when Forrest just barely shook his head, he didn't say anything. Adina was Forrest's patient. His responsibility. And he'd failed to see the choice she had clearly been going to make.

Adina swallowed but didn't confirm or deny what he was saying. "Mark doesn't have anyone. His ex-wife got all the friends in the divorce, not that he minds. He's a loner."

"He has you."

Sam's interruption was rewarded with a swift glare.

"Yes. And when he has surgery, he is going to need someone there." She flinched as she moved her leg.

The infection they'd been so worried about in Mark was now second to the one crawling through Adina's system.

"I'm admitting you." Forrest's tone was harsh this time. He was not going to accept any argument. If he let her go and this worsened, and it would, her life was in danger.

"I'm fine." Adina raised her chin, but the wobbling lips were still there.

"You are not." Forrest shook his head. "I failed to realize you were a danger to yourself last time. But you are, which means we are allowed to hold you here against your will. Don't make me file that paperwork."

He looked at Sam. The frustration was clear in his eyes, but his face was serene. Good. He could play the role of good doctor, a sympathetic ear to listen to Adina, while Forrest took on the role of ass to make sure she got the care she needed.

She looked at the door, clearly questioning how serious the threat Forrest had issued was.

"If you are admitted, it will be easier for me to get you on the evac plane." Sam's calm words made Adina let out a breath.

"It hurts." She bit her lip. "I didn't think it would get this bad. Two days ago it was just really warm and sore, but now..."

Forrest put one arm under her left shoulder and Sam followed on the right side. "We need to take a look and get an intravenous antibiotic started immediately."

Sam looked over her head. "I will call Houston as soon as we get you to the bed. Forrest can evaluate."

"So you'll tell them it's for two?" She hiccupped the words out as tears started down her cheeks.

"Forrest is right. You are a danger to yourself, if you stay." He helped Forrest get her into the bed and then walked off.

"I didn't mean to put myself in danger." Adina pushed away a tear. "Not really. It happened so fast. I just need to be on that plane with him. He needs someone to look after him at home. He has no one else."

Forrest nodded as he looked at the burn. The red streaks were light but clearly headed toward lymph nodes. He took her temperature, not surprised to find it elevated.

Lymphangitis. Dangerous and fast moving, but treatable.

"It's painful to the touch and there is discharge. I'm starting an antibiotic, now." Forrest went to grab the IV bag and the needle he needed.

It would be nice if one of the NPs was here. People complained sometimes that they wanted their doctor to place the IV. Forrest was capable, but it was routine for nurses. They were the experts.

But all Adina had was him. So, he found the vein and got the bag hung. Set her leg up in elevation and took a deep breath. "I am going to give you a sedative because I'm guessing you didn't sleep last night."

"No." She pursed her lips. "Thank you, Doc Two."

Forrest administered the sedative then walked over to where Sam was on the Wi-Fi phone.

"Seven hours? I'll have both of them prepped. I

know I said one this morning, but you are sending the plane anyway. If she stays here without him, she's a danger to herself."

Forrest wrote on a note and passed it over.

It's lymphangitis.

Sam raised a brow and passed the information on to the person on the other end. "There were streaks headed toward the lymph nodes this morning. There is drainage and clear infection." He pinched his eyes closed as he listened to whatever the person was saying on the end of the phone.

"I know this is unorthodox, but so is having a patient evacced. This is not a normal situation and he needs surgery as soon as possible." He tapped his free hand against the desk, eyes still closed.

Forrest reached out, putting his hand over his. Sam let out a breath and looked at him. He mouthed *Thank you* as he listened to whatever was being said on the other side of the world.

This was frustrating. But it was far from the first frustration Sam had handled in his career. Growing up, Forrest had watched television shows about doctors and the nurses working beside them. The dramas were always nerve-rattling. The diagnoses rare and terrifying.

It made for good television but did not give an accurate representation of life in a medical setting. You fought with insurance companies who thought they knew more about what was happening than the physician with the patient in front of them. Fought with administration about resources. Stuff that did not make for good television but was the everyday reality.

It added more stress to an already stressful job.

"Thank you. We'll get *them* prepped." Sam's blue eyes met Forrest's as he said *them* and held his gaze. "Separating them is not a good idea. They aren't lovers, but they love each other."

The words spun around them. They were about Adina and Mark. But maybe...just maybe there was another message there, too.

CHAPTER NINE

THE WIND WHIPPED around them as they watched the operators of the C-130 wave as the door to the plane on skis closed. The US Air Force 109th Airlift Wing operated the plane that could land in the most inhospitable place on the planet. There were a doctor and nurse on the plane who were now in charge of Mark and Adina's care.

Sam and Forrest's jobs were done. They'd given Mark his best-case scenario. With any luck he'd be in surgery a few hours after he landed.

And Adina. Forrest pursed his lips as the plane engines revved in preparation for takeoff.

She was going to be okay. Though it was possible she'd need a skin graft too, if the infection spread any more. He should have seen the possibility. Should have suspected.

There were signs. And he'd missed them. Chalked her statements up to jokes. To banter. And now she was on the plane, with her best friend, as a patient herself.

If she'd talked to him, to Sam, maybe they could have figured something else out. Mentally harping on it wasn't doing him any good.

"This is the second evac we've stood next to each other at. Hopefully they get the same good news Dr. Anderson got." Forrest shouted the words as the plane headed down the ice runway and took off. At least this was a topic to clear his mind. Dr. Anderson had a long road to recovery, but he'd emailed and said his oncologist expected him to make a full recovery. With any luck, in a couple of weeks they'd get similar updates on Mark and Adina.

"Yeah, but this one is very different," Sam shouted back as he motioned for them to head back.

Very different? Hardly.

"Not really. Double the patients, sure, and more dangerous for the ones on the plane but otherwise same deal. Patients need evacuation and we are out in the cold." Forrest lowered his voice as the plane's roar disappeared into the dark sky.

"Yeah, but we're talking now." Sam rolled his shoulders, cringing as they got up by his ears.

Good point. "I told you you'd be sore if you didn't stop rowing this morning." Flutters danced through Forrest's stomach as he tried to keep his focus on something other than the hot man next to him.

You wanted to think of something other than your patients. Mission accomplished.

"You did. You were right. I am tight as a spring." They walked into the dorm area. Sam's room was down the left hall, and Forrest's was down the right.

"Want to hang out for a little while? I'm exhausted, but my brain's not going to shut down after the day we've had. You can come to my room. I have a little couch area. I've got some beers in the fridge." Forrest wasn't sure where the offer came from.

Except he was. His heart wanted Sam. Wanted time with him.

They'd kissed this morning. How could one twenty-four-hour period be so long and so short? The smart move might be to put a bit of distance between them. But distance was the thing Forrest wanted least in this world.

"Sure." Sam grinned. "But let me go to my room and get into comfier clothes."

"Good plan." Forrest nodded and walked down to his room. There was no sense trying to ignore the butterflies dancing around his stomach.

He got to his place, stripped and put on some comfortable pajama pants and a soft blue T-shirt. He grabbed the beers from his fridge. McMurdo allowed the station residents to purchase an alcohol ration each week. Forrest made little use of his allotted amount. But that meant he had a decent stash for hosting.

Not that he'd ever hosted anyone in his room.

The clock ticked past ten minutes and Forrest tried not to ignore the tiny voice whispering that Sam had changed his mind. It wasn't a huge deal if that was the case.

Except it was.

Forrest closed his eyes and took a deep breath.

"What will be will be." The mantra was one his therapist had recommended, but it didn't bring any relief as the door to his room stayed un-knocked-on.

Another deep breath, another quiet moment.

Then a swift knock.

Forrest let out the breath he very much knew he'd been holding. He strode to the door, opened it and his heart sang as Sam stood on the other side.

His hair was damp and he smelled like the shampoo that had been in their shower for so long.

"Sorry." Sam shrugged and winced. "The shower took longer than planned because raising my hands over my head was painful." He took the beer Forrest offered and took a deep sip. "Guess I was running on adrenaline to get Mark on the plane, because I didn't feel it as we were loading him."

Forrest wasn't surprised by the admission. The body could ignore a lot when it was running on stress. And injured muscles liked heat, but only after the initial inflammation died down. "You overextended yourself this morning. Heat was the worst thing for the muscles. You need to ice them."

"Forgive me for not wanting to ice anything when we are surrounded by the ice all the time." Sam took another drink. "Guess I'm not great company."

"You are fine company." Forrest set his beer down and stood. "And I seem to remember the best cure for this anyway." He stepped behind Sam and put his hands on his shoulders.

Pressing his thumb into the pressure points, he wasn't surprised when Sam let out a grunt. "You're stiffer than I imagined."

"That was something you used to joke with me about." Sam chuckled at the old innuendo.

"That wasn't exactly how I put it." Forrest dug into Sam's shoulders with his thumb. Yes, the massage would break up the knots he'd created with the oversized workout, but it would also teach him a good lesson about such jokes.

"Ouch." Sam looked back over the chair, his jeweled gaze gripping Forrest. "I earned that."

"Do you want the massage or do you want to go to bed sore?"

"I think we are both going to bed sore, but yes. Thank you." Sam leaned back up and sighed as Forrest worked through the knots on his shoulders.

"You should make sure you take some pain reliever tonight. Anti-inflammatories." It was advice Sam didn't need.

"Yes, Doc Two." Sam chuckled and drained the last of his beer. "I should get going." He stood and moved around the couch.

Forrest didn't argue. The room was hot. Crispy with tension. And if Sam stayed any longer, he'd act. Just like he had this morning.

Sam hadn't brought up the kiss. The innuendo-laden jokes were little pitfalls on the way to the giant landmine they seemed to be dancing around.

"I hope you sleep well." Forrest took a deep breath as Sam stepped a little closer. The scent of him was going to stain the room for the next several hours.

Thank God.

Sam leaned toward him and Forrest waited for the connection he saw in his eyes. Instead, Sam dropped his beer in the waste bin behind him.

"What are we doing?" Forrest wasn't sure the question had actually made it out of his mouth until Sam paused.

Their lips were inches from each other.

"You were the one that kissed me this morning. You tell me." Sam's body heat pressed against Forrest.

"I don't know." That was the truth. He wasn't sure what this was. What it wasn't. They were at the end of the earth, literally. Trapped together. There was no plan here.

"Me, either." Sam whispered, then closed the distance between them.

This kiss was slow. Not the passionate rampage of this morning. Sam's mouth pressed against his as he ran one hand up Forrest's back and stroked his cheek with the other.

A worshipful remembrance.

"Sam." He breathed out the name. Locked in the sanctity of the moment.

"Forrest."

His name on Sam's lips. His body tightened and his soul ignited. Damn he'd missed him. Missed the jokes. The talks. The passionate kisses and these moments.

Him. He'd just missed Sam.

The kiss continued, or maybe time stopped to allow them everything they needed.

When Sam finally broke the moment and stepped back, Forrest put his hands to his lips, staring at the man. No words breaking forth.

"Good night, Forrest." Sam smiled and headed for the door. "And thanks for the massage."

The door was closed before Forrest could say good night.

Or beg him to stay.

***

"Earth to Sam." Nat waved a hand in front of his face, as she stood in front of him.

Sam blinked. The nurse worked night shift back in the States, but he hadn't been aware she moved like shadows. "Sorry, my brain slipped out a moment when I didn't see you here."

Slipped out was not even a lie. With no one around, Sam's mind had hopped to the kiss he'd planted on Forrest three days ago.

A lifetime ago.

She raised a brow and pointed to the currently empty bays. "I figured that you'd enjoy a restocked unit to start the shift with."

"Not an incorrect assumption." Sam grinned, grateful she hadn't asked for details about his wandering thoughts.

"Given the week we've had, you're entitled to more than a moment of daydreaming." She let out a breath.

"Was last night rough then?" Since they'd deposited Adina and Mark on the C-130, the clinic had had a steady stream of patients. All minor things, thankfully. But no restful periods. Which for a station holding only a few hundred people was surprising.

"Not rough, just continuous." She pulled up the tablet. "All of it was standard. Stitches for a scientist who slipped on the ice. Two with headaches so bad they were having trouble sleeping and a case of insomnia."

"Insomnia is something we are likely going see an uptick in. It's a common complaint here." And something people had a tendency not to report. But it could cause a multitude of health conditions.

Natasha sighed as she looked out the small window near the front door. "I love working the night shift at home. My friends joke that I live for the night. But twenty-four-hour darkness messes with you."

She pushed her finger along the tablet. "The good news is no new admissions. Chris and I were able to patch everyone up or administer medication and release them. So."

Sam chucked as she ended the sentences on a word others might expect to have follow-on commentary attached to. Natasha was an ER nurse. He was an ER doctor. Both of them were superstitious enough not to mention a quiet morning.

No need to tempt fates already seemingly hell bent on overworking the limited medical staff in residence.

"Forrest coming in today?"

Natasha didn't look up from her scrolling as she said it. Still, he thought he heard the hint of another question there. He knew there were questions about the pair of them. How could there not be? When they were not in the clinic, they could usually be found together.

McMurdo Station was basically a small town and rumors kept the boredom at bay. Or at least lightened the doldrums.

"He'll stop by, but he needs to get some stuff done in the lab." Sam hadn't broached the topic of their kiss in Forrest's room. The soft, exploratory connection that seemed fierier than the one in the gym. His brain kept replaying the moment.

He hadn't brought it up. And neither had Forrest. It was a weird limbo hovering over their morning workouts and mealtimes. An undiscussed boulder that Sam kept waffling between bringing up and burying deep inside.

The only thing he couldn't do was forget it.

"He's working two jobs. He needs to be careful." Nat yawned as she passed the tablet to Sam. "All yours."

Sam took the tablet and asked, "Careful, how?" Had she seen something he hadn't? A problem he'd missed because he was focusing on Forrest's lips and perfectly sculpted body?

"I worked here three winters ago. It can be easy to work constantly. To lose track of how much stress you are putting on your body. The constant darkness and limited activities do something to your brain. Make it forget, or depress, the stress its dealing with. I've seen more than one scientist crack." She yawned, again. "He's probably fine, but you should just keep an eye on him. Not that that will be hard, right?"

She winked and walked toward the door before Sam could mutter any kind of response. He looked around the room, the quiet room… At least he could use this time to catch up on a doctor's worst nightmare—paperwork.

"Sorry I took so long." Forrest shook the snowflakes from his head as he stepped into the clinic. "The lab results all seemed to come together at once."

"We aren't anticipating another outbreak, are we?" Sam's day had included two individuals with colds that had created serious sinus infections. Both were incredibly uncomfortable, but he didn't think they were super contagious.

"No. At least not one that the results are predicting. I mean it could happen—we have a lot of people living in close proximity. And even when you don't the odds are always greater than zero with germs."

"Geez, Forrest." Sam shook his head, "Doom and gloom much?"

"What?" Forrest's dark eyes were sparkling as the tips of his lips tried to keep from forming a full smile.

Sam tilted his head, "You know what. I get that you look at germs all day. That you test individuals at random around the base. And of course you have those boxes all around this place. I know you are excited by those results, but the ER physician—" Sam pointed to himself and ignored the chuckle coming from Forrest "—hears germs, population density discussion and odds not zero and his nervous system starts to race."

"That is why you never showed any interest in internal medicine or epidemiology." Forrest stepped a little closer.

Heat erupted across Sam's skin. The temperature rising had nothing to do with the "scary" topic Forrest was discussing and everything to do with the six-foot Adonis that haunted every single dream these days.

Forrest stopped at the edge of the desk and looked

toward the empty bays. "Looks like you didn't really need me today."

Sam let out a breath, as he looked at the empty beds too, grateful Forrest hadn't used the dreaded word *quiet*.

Forrest must have noticed. "I chose internal medicine and then the lab, but I rotated through the ER. I know better than to mention certain things." He leaned against the desk, looking hotter than any man had a right to.

"It was steady but no one needed admitting. Natasha said she and Chris had the same last night. That is the pattern I was told to expect."

The front door of the clinic opened and both men turned as a petite redhead walked in. Tears were frozen on her cheeks.

Forrest was closer than Sam was and reached her first. "What's wrong? What hurts?"

"My heart, and no, I am not having a heart attack." The young woman wiped away fresh tears as she looked between the men. "I need medication for depression. There I said it." She blew out a breath then pinched her eyes closed.

"All right." Forrest gestured to an empty bed. "Come tell us what's going on."

"I *told* you. I need de… de… Damn it! I just said the words."

"Depression meds?" Sam helped out and was stunned to see Forrest's gaze cut to him. The man gave him a subtle shake of the head.

"What do you need?" Forrest took the woman's

coat from her and hung it across a chair. She hadn't bothered to hang it on the hooks by the door, probably because she was too focused on getting in and getting out the words that she considered so hard.

One of the toughest issues for Sam in the ER was explaining to family members, first responders and others that mental health care was needed as much as trauma surgery or oncologists. The stigma behind it was why the woman on the bed was struggling so much.

"He said the words." She pointed at Sam.

"I know." Forrest offered a gentle smile. "But I need you to talk about what you need and why. I've taken medication for anxiety and depression. I have a therapist that I still meet with over email while I'm here. There is nothing wrong with asking for help. But being able to ask is the first step."

Damn, he was good at this.

"I need medication for—" she cut her eyes to Sam in mute appeal, but he shook his head.

Forrest was right. She needed to ask. Needed to accept that this was what she was struggling with and that there was nothing wrong with that.

"Depression." She bent her head and let out a sob.

"All right." Forrest grabbed a chart from the wall. "Let's start with the basics, your name?"

"Megan Pauli." She hiccupped. "If life was fair, it would be Megan Smith. How silly is that? I wanted, craved, such a bland last name. But it was…" Her words died away in a sob.

Sam understood the heartache happening here.

"What is today the anniversary of?" The day he'd had marked on his calendar to wed Oliver he'd packed his bags and moved across the country, determined not to look more than a few months into his future. And he still made sure to work overtime on the anniversary of the day he and Forrest first kissed. A date that was coming up.

"My fiancé's birthday. He died a year ago. I came here because..." She shrugged.

"Because it was easier than staying home." Sam finished what she couldn't say.

She nodded.

He understood. He'd taken to the road for the same reasons.

Forrest looked at him, just a quick glance, then back at Megan. "Have you ever taken medication for depression?"

"No. My mother, well, she told me to just get over it. Work and not think. And it was working."

"No." Sam shook his head. "It wasn't. You were just putting off the support your body needs. And no one should tell you how to handle your grief."

Megan bit her lip so hard Sam worried she might be tasting blood. "I loved Dillon so much. I thought I knew how lucky I was, but now, now I wish I could go back in time and tell that version of me to soak up every moment. Because I had no idea what I had when I had it."

Forrest's gaze met Sam's again, for just a moment. "All right, since you've never used depression medication, we are going to start on the lowest dose. These medications take time to work as they build up in your system. I want to check back in two weeks on how they are working, but it will be a full thirty days before you enjoy all the effects."

"In the meantime, we are going to set you up with weekly therapy appointments." Sam would email Houston and make sure they found someone who could use the telehealth system so Megan could talk to someone who wouldn't tell her to bury her emotions. Who would just let her be.

Forrest got the meds and went over the requirements, possible side effects. Sam stood to the side. Unneeded in this moment. Lost in Megan's simple words.

I had no idea what I had when I had it.

Sam's eyes fell on Forrest. His heart, his mind, everything had made sense when they were together. And nothing had truly fit since they separated.

"Eh! Megan. Glad you made it in." Chris raised a hand as Sam turned. "I recommended she visit, glad you did. Want to go over notes so you can head out of here, Doc?"

"Yes." Sam wanted out of there. But for the first time in forever he also knew where he wanted to go.

CHAPTER TEN

FORREST DIDN'T TRY to stop his feet from moving down the hall. He wasn't giving himself time to think this through. Megan's words had haunted him as he'd showered. Echoed through him as he threw on his clothes. Followed him with every step he took.

He needed Sam. It was as simple, and as complicated, as that.

Reaching the door, Forrest didn't hesitate to raise his hand, but before he could knock, Sam opened the door.

"Oh, good."

Forrest wasn't sure what he'd expected Sam to say, but that wasn't it.

Sam reached for his shirt and pulled him in. "I was just on my way to you." He closed the door and took a deep breath. "Forrest."

His hands cupped Forrest's cheek. His thumb running across his cheek. "You're a little scruffy."

His smile sent lightning bolts through Forrest. "You said you liked it." He'd picked up the razor in the shower, then set it aside. Years of being instructed to keep a shaven face. Decades of shaving in the morning and at night. But Sam's words had echoed in his head.

"I do like it." Sam's free hand ran along Forrest's stomach.

His groin hardened and need pushed against every

nerve. His body was a lightning rod, specifically designed for the man in front of him. "Sam."

"I love how you say my name. I always did."

Before Forrest could react to that statement, Sam's mouth was on his. The kiss jolted him. His hands were on Sam's body, tracing paths his mind knew by memory.

He broke the kiss and bent his head to the crook of Sam's neck. He swept his tongue across the skin and was rewarded with Sam gripping his ass.

"Tease." Sam's husky voice whispered into his ear.

"There is no tease here." Forrest put his hands on either side of Sam's face. "I want you. I need you."

"You have no idea how many dreams I've woken from just after you've said those words." Sam dragged a finger along Forrest's stomach.

Forrest hated that admission. "I'm here now."

"You're here now." Sam repeated the words before grazing Forrest's mouth with his lips.

"Who's the tease, now?" Forrest pulled Sam against him, very aware of how turned on they each were. Their hips pressed together, their bodies reacquainting with each other.

Forrest craved this man and was fighting every urge to devour him. He was not rushing a single moment of this.

Sam's hands gripped Forrest's and pushed them over his head as he captured Forrest's mouth with his own. Being pressed up against a door, with his lover worshiping his lips was certainly a match for any fantasy Forrest's mind had managed to conjure up. Each stroke of Sam's tongue stirred the flame the first sight of him on the ship had ignited. The ember that had refused to die. "Sam."

Sam released his hands and he took the opportunity to lift Sam's shirt over his head. As if in answer, Sam's fingers gripped his shirt and ripped it from his body.

Forrest took a deep breath as his former lover stared at his body.

The man in front of him could have been an Olympian, but he'd put that goal aside to focus on med school. But while his six-pack wasn't as defined as it had been in college, it was still there.

Forrest still worked out, but he was not as toned as he'd been. And then there were the tattoos. The last time they lain together his skin had contained no ink.

Now his stomach and his back were etched with pictures. Memories. Things he'd never be able to let go. Images carefully picked but placed where no one ever saw them. Only the tattoo artists had ever glimpsed them.

Sam's finger ran over the Christmas tree over his right bicep. "This one makes sense." He looked at the phoenix stretched across his abdomen. "This one, too." He kissed the words on his collarbone. "I hate that I understand why you have this one, too." His tongue flicked along the phrase.

"It was the first one I got." Two weeks after he'd walked away from Sam. The words *We're All Mad Here* were meant to make him feel like he'd made the right choice. It hadn't worked. But it had created a need to continue to modify his body.

Sam's touch feathered along the waistband of his pants and Forrest's groin tightened. "Any others?"

"Not there." Forrest winked as he reached for Sam. He was too turned on to let the ink he'd placed on his body distract him from the Adonis before him.

Sam's hand slid along Forrest's length. There were two layers of fabric between his palm and Forrest's skin, but still need nearly drove him to his knees.

"Turn." The order echoed in the room. "I want to see the others. I find that ink turns me on."

Forrest lightly traced a finger along Sam's erection, enjoying the groan echoing from his lips. He let his touch linger for just a moment before turning.

His back piece was a road. With a man walking a broken path between woods and ocean. It was the signature piece in the artist's portfolio.

Sam's body pressed against his. "Any on your tight ass?"

"One way to find out."

His pants and boxers disappeared with record speed. Sam gripped his very tattoo-less butt.

"No tats, but still hot as hell." Sam massaged his butt before slipping between his legs and cupping his balls. He stroked Forrest's length but their position against the door kept Forrest from moving with the touch.

It was torture and explicit pleasure all wrapped in one.

Every nerve ending was pulsing and Forrest had

had enough. "Sam..." Before he could finish the plea, Sam gripped his shoulders and spun him around.

Then he slid to the ground and took Forrest in his mouth. The heat, the longing, the need, all of it hit him as Sam gripped his ass, pulling him closer.

Forrest closed his eyes and let Sam take him fully over the edge.

Sam stood, grinning as Forrest's eyes darkened in the aftermath of his orgasm. "Forrest."

"My turn."

Forrest had captured Sam's mouth and was guiding them toward the bed before Sam could utter another word. Not that he had much interest in saying anything else when Forrest was taking charge.

Forrest wasn't soft. Wasn't hesitant. His hands were cascading over Sam's body, touching all the places guaranteed to make him come undone.

When Sam's knees hit the edge of his bed, Forrest reached his arm around his back to stop him from falling backward. "I am completely naked," Forrest purred.

"Trust me, I know." Sam's gaze slid over the phoenix on Forrest's belly. He hadn't been kidding. The tattoos were a huge turn-on. He'd never cared about tattoos. He'd been with men who were covered in them and those who had none. They'd never registered as anything significant.

But on Forrest... The hidden gems were catnip to an already greedy need.

Forrest's hand slipped into his loose sweats and Sam sighed as it slid around his length.

"You still don't wear boxers to bed." Forrest pressed kisses along his neck, pausing at the exact spot that never failed to elicit a moan from Sam.

This was new. *And* familiar.

Forrest yanked on the drawstring of Sam's sweats, grinning as the pants hit the floor. His palm splayed across Sam's chest as he pressed him back on the bed.

Forrest's lips drifted along his inner thighs as his fingers teased ever closer to the aching length. Sam gripped the sheets as Forrest's tongue trailed along his thigh, over his balls and finally to where he craved him most.

Sam woke to Forrest shifting in the bed next to him. There wasn't much room and it reminded him of the first night they'd fallen asleep together in a college dorm.

"We haven't slept in such a confined space since college." Forrest sighed but made no move to exit the bed.

Dropping a hand around Forrest's waist, Sam kissed his shoulder, where a bird in flight was imprinted. "I was just thinking the same thing." He ran a hand over Forrest's stomach.

There was nothing sexual about the motion. It was a simple touch. One he'd missed so much. Oliver hadn't liked to snuggle. In fact, the man had insisted on a king-size bed so there was no chance of rolling into each other at night.

One of many red flags Sam had ignored in his pursuit of perfect love. This wasn't perfect, though. It was—well—they'd never discussed what it was. In fact when asked directly, Forrest had said he didn't know.

Sam wasn't going to press. Once upon a time he would have. Would have spent hours, days running through his life plan. Plotted the next year, five, forever.

That man was gone. This Sam spent his life moving from one thing to the next. This was an adventure and when the winter was over, the next adventure would begin.

That didn't mean he wasn't going to soak up every moment he had now.

"Why the tattoos?" He ran a hand over where he knew the phoenix was. "You never mentioned anything about wanting ink. And you have a lot. All carefully hidden."

Forrest's body lifted as he chuckled. "The first was a fluke. I got it to feel something. Which sounds ridiculous, but I was so lost and unsure what my next steps should be." He let out a sigh.

Was he waiting for Sam to ask when that was? To press? Dozens of questions pummeled his brain but he didn't ask a single one.

"I saw a flash sale at a place I was walking by. Fifty bucks as long as it was something from the sheet they had. The *We're All Mad Here* line stuck out. I was never much for classic literature. Guess my grandmother refusing to read to me as a kid left some holes in my book knowledge. It wasn't until I saw a video on a social media site years later that I realized it was a quote from *Alice in Wonderland*."

"It's the Cheshire cat's line. At least in the book." Sam pressed a kiss to Forrest's shoulder.

Forrest shifted; his ass running along Sam's length. "Show-off."

Sam hardened, but he was not going to give in to that. Not yet. "Forrest doing something on a whim. Wow."

"Yeah. Well, that was the only one I did on a whim. But you'll hear people say that once they have one, they must have more. I got the phoenix on the anniversary of my grandmother's death."

Sam chuckled, "She would not have liked that."

Forrest rolled over; his face so close to Sam's own. "She would not. But that was the point."

"And the Christmas tree?" Sam ran a hand over the tree, then felt his mouth fall open as he took a full look at it. "The topper."

Forrest pursed his lips, as his hands stroked Sam's side. "Yeah."

It was their tree topper. A chintzy angel missing one wing. They'd found it at a holiday bazaar as freshman in college. The friendship days.

It had come with them to every room, then apartment. Sitting on top of their tree and starting conversations with anyone that saw it. It was buried in the back of the closet at Sam's parents' place with all the other things from that life that he couldn't seem to toss out.

"Another whim?" Maybe it was an unfair question. But Forrest had been the one to walk out. The one who said he didn't know what this was when Sam had asked the other night.

He was the one that showed up here last night.
But I was going to him, too.

Sam forced the argument from his brain. He wanted this answer. Needed Forrest's response to this.

"No." Forrest placed a hand on his cheek. "I showed the artists the picture. Told him the story about how we found it and had to haggle with the woman over the price."

Sam couldn't stop the grin that reminder brought. "I can't believe she wanted to charge us full price for a broken tree topper."

That tree topper meant something. A memory Forrest had permanently cemented on his body. He'd kept the memory, but not the man tied to it.

"She drove a hard bargain." Forrest's lips traced his. A soft touch, barely there.

But enough to force the hurt back into the recesses of Sam's mind.

"She did." Sam slipped a hand up Forrest's thigh, skimming close to his growing erection but not touching it. "Not as hard as you."

Forrest's fingers wrapped around his length. "You're one to talk."

Sam captured Forrest's mouth. This was what he wanted to focus on. The present. The man in his bed right now.

CHAPTER ELEVEN

"It's weird working with you." Chris pushed the cart of supplies over to the bay where he and Sam were finishing up inventory while they had a lull in patients. "Not that I mind. Just weird."

"Missing Natasha?" Sam shrugged. "Is she a better colleague than me?"

"She is." Chris winked. "But only because the woman never stops moving."

"What I hear is that you can sit back while she does all the work." Sam raised a brow, mostly joking but also wanting to make sure that Nat wasn't getting stuck with more than her share of the workload. He and Forrest had worked the same shift for the entire time Mark had needed care.

And if he was being honest, he'd prefer working with Forrest over Chris and Nat, too.

"No. I just mean there is no sitting back with her." Chris put the bandages in the cabinet. "I've spent my career in big-city trauma units. There is no down time. I mean none. I actually came here because I needed a chance to relax, but here..."

Chris looked at the door, holding his breath for a second.

"I don't think you can just wish for a patient and have them magically walk through the door." Sam understood Chris's trouble. The first time he'd landed at a rural hospital he'd gone two nights with barely any patients. After years of spending every moment of a shift running from emergency to emergency, the quiet had nearly driven him mad.

"I'm not wishing for one." Chris blew out a breath. "Not really."

"Uh-huh. Careful what you wish for." Sam's third night at that first hospital had gone to hell almost as soon as he'd walked in the door. A capsized fishing boat with two families with small children. Nightmare fuel. He'd never resented a slow night again.

"I know. I know. I just never thought I'd miss it. The chaos. The adrenaline. The pain. The excitement. That probably sounds terrible." Chris cleared his throat and started toward the desk, "What's next on the agenda?"

"Chris..." Sam pushed the now-empty cart of supplies to the side. "There is nothing wrong with realizing that you aren't cut out for certain kinds of work. It isn't a failure to find you don't like something."

"Yeah. Natasha said the same thing." He looked at the computer and sat down. "I might as well catch up on my charting." He let out a chuckle that wasn't quite happy. "Words I never thought I'd say. Right now, I think of charting as a way to pass the time. Weird."

"I get it." Sam looked at the currently empty clinic, "I'm going to run a quick errand. I have the walkie-talkie if you need me."

"I'm going to do my best not to want to need you." Chris started typing, his eyes glued to the screen.

There were still nearly four months to go on this winter rotation. With any luck there were more long, boring days in front of them. And that meant Chris was going to struggle. Sam made a mental note to keep an eye on him in case the stress needed to be addressed.

After pushing through the snow, Sam arrived at the building housing Forrest's lab. They'd spent the last three nights together. He hadn't been this happy in years. They hadn't talked about the future, though. No discussion on what was next. No planning. Despite that, Sam was determined to soak it in. Enjoy all the moments before they headed in different directions again.

He knocked on Forrest's lab door and entered when he heard Charlee call out.

"You don't have to knock. This isn't a secure lab." The woman grinned before turning back to her microscope. "He's in the back with the graphs and charts." She made a noise at the end of the sentence that made Sam pretty sure Charlee felt the same way about statistics as he did.

He'd met a surprising number of scientists and doctors alike, that loved the science but hated the metrics. Forrest had always enjoyed both. It was why he was so good at internal medicine. And yet, according to Forrest himself, he was hiding that skill away in a lab.

He was standing looking at a giant white board crammed into the side of the lab. There were notes, formulas and a Venn diagram in the corner.

Forrest was so intent on the science on the board

that Sam didn't want to interrupt. So he took advantage and let his eyes roam.

Forrest had his hand on his chin. His unshaved chin. Sam's belly tightened at that small detail. It would be so easy to pretend that it meant something deep. Meant he could start thinking of the future, after they got off this ice rock.

He just isn't shaving that often. Don't run away with ideas. Don't start planning forever with a man who's never mentioned it.

"You going to say anything or are you just here to stare at my ass?" Forrest didn't turn or shift his position at the board, but Sam could hear the smile on his lips.

"I wasn't staring at your ass." It was an incredible butt. Majestic even. But Sam hadn't even darted an eye toward it.

Forrest turned his head, his eyes wide, "Should I be concerned then? Three nights together and you're already uninterested in my backside?"

Sam looked toward the section where Charlee was working. Forrest was always serious at work. Focused. It was what made him such a good internist.

"She wears headphones. With music turned up so loud I have to nearly scream, or step on the light sensor she keeps on the floor next to her station so she doesn't get a jump scare when I'm getting her attention."

"She heard me knock." Sam looked back towards Charlee clearly bopping along to the beat of whatever was in the headset.

"No she didn't. Charlee installed a sensor on the floor by the lab's door, too. It sets off a green light so she knows someone is there. Pretty brilliant." Forrest winked, then turned back to the board. "But it means she really can't hear you; so feel free to compliment my butt to your heart's content."

"I really wasn't looking at your butt, though it is a very nice ass and I am far from tired of it, Forrest." Sam walked over to the board, not exactly sure what he was looking at. "What is all this?"

"The viral load of most of the base. The changes over the last two months. The shifts. Though it's too early to really see major differences. You can see the shift when the stomach virus went through the post." Forrest pointed to a graph he'd taped to the board. "And this week's shift." He pointed to another graph.

"Anything we should be concerned about?" Sam hadn't expected to have in-depth access to advance information on what was plaguing the residents, but he'd take it.

"No. And all of it's randomized anyway. Except for that." He pointed to the graph from the virus load. "Which is Charlee and me. The base knows about the collection points Charlee and I set up around the area. They swab their mouth and their nose, put the date on the sample and place it in the collection site."

"Even randomized, it still shows spikes."

"It does." Forrest turned completely around. "Not that I don't love talking about the study I'm doing, but that is not why you are here."

There was no point in denying it. "No. I came to talk clinic schedules."

"Oh." Forrest shook his head, "Right. I should have stopped by this morning to see where you wanted me in the rotation. With Mark and Adina being gone, I assume it will be more of an 'as needed' schedule versus standard rotation."

That made the most sense. Forrest had work to do. The reason he was at the pole. The study he and Charlee were contracted to deliver.

"I mean, we won't need you as often, but I would still like to have you there at least three shifts a week. That way the NPs can get a break." Maybe Forrest would remember why he was such a good fit for bedside if he worked a few extra shifts. Stop hiding.

"What about you? When do you get a break?"

He didn't. But that was something Sam was used to. He took breaks when the clinic was slow. It was a trick he'd learned since taking on rotations in rural places where he was often the lone doc on duty. "I was hired as the primary doc. I'll rest when this is over. For now, my nurses need, and deserve, to spend time elsewhere. On the plus side, they both prefer to work night shift."

Selfishly, he wanted Forrest in the clinic full-time. What a change from the start of the winter session. And it wasn't only because Sam loved his company and was sleeping with him. Though those two things didn't hurt.

Forrest was great at the clinic. At bedside. He'd

left the bedside because of some bad experiences. But bad experiences were part of medicine.

He was an excellent doctor. And honestly, there were far too few of those in the world. He should be seeing patients. Not stuffed away in a lab answering to white boards and statistics.

"I can do that. Or four shifts. Though not sure I am the best help. I missed Adina's—"

"Nope." Sam held up a hand, stopping that statement. It had been a patient going south that had pushed Forrest into the lab in the first place. Sam was not letting him focus on Adina in the same way. "*We* missed Adina."

"I was her doctor." Forrest started to turn back to his board.

Sam closed the distance between them and spun the other man around. "*We* were her doctors. I missed it, too. I was so focused on Mark that I didn't see the concern. It is my clinic—"

"Nope." Now it was Forrest interrupting him. "No. It is not your clinic. You're stationed here. It's the Center for Polar Medical Operations' clinic. You are their employee. And you need to be getting rest, too."

"Geez." Charlee rounded the corner. "Even with my headphones on I can hear you two arguing. And the answer is so freaking easy."

Forrest tilted his head. "And what is the easy answer, Charlee?"

"Just kiss already. I mean, seriously." She rolled her eyes to the ceiling.

"Yeah. That's already been taken care of, Charlee.

But I appreciate the input." Forrest crossed his arms but color was stealing up his cheeks.

"Oh. Then why the hell is there still so much sexual tension between the two of you? Maybe you need to do more than kiss." She put her headphones back on and made a show of turning the volume up before stamping away.

"I don't think we need to tell her that that has already been taken care of. Do you?" Sam couldn't stop his grin as he felt his own cheeks heat.

Forrest looked around him, making certain Charlee was gone, before pressing a quick kiss to Sam's lips. His fingers grazed Sam's cheek before he shook his head. "No. I don't think we need to give her all that detail. Put me on the schedule, let me know who I am working with and when I need to show up."

Sam leaned in, enjoying the soft scent of Forrest's shampoo. "You're working with me." Then he kissed his cheek and turned on his heel before he could run the risk of fully kissing Forrest, even with Charlee on the other side of the lab.

Forrest smiled at a passing couple on their way to movie night. He was headed in the other direction; he and Sam had agreed to join Charlee and her friend Tina for trivia night in the canteen.

The last week had been blissful. Even if he was starting to feel like he was burning his candle on both ends and a little down the middle. He worked in the lab for several hours early in the morning. Then a shift at the clinic. Then hung out with Sam.

"Hey." Sam caught up to him and slid his arm around Forrest's shoulders. "You snuck out again this morning."

"I needed to check on some things in the lab." Forrest caught the yawn that was pressing against the back of his throat. He'd learned to work through exhaustion in college. High school, really. He'd had a job from the moment he looked sixteen, which was a little before he turned fifteen. So he'd shown up to a job, then gone to school, done homework, then more work and a few hours of sleep. It had been great preparation for residency.

Since he'd taken his lab position, his body had gotten used to enjoying six to eight hours of uninterrupted sleep. But it would readjust. Until then, he'd just make sure the mask he'd perfected in med school was on all the time so no one knew how close to the edge he was.

"Right. The lab." Before Forrest could ask what Sam meant by the tone he used, he was already moving on, "You ready to kick some butt at trivia night?"

Forrest pressed a kiss to Sam's forehead as they walked into the canteen. "I'm here for the company and the ice cream. I don't think we need to kick butt to have a good time."

"Speak for yourself." Sam squeezed his shoulder before letting go. "Though I am looking forward to the ice cream. Is it weird that we're living in a frozen wasteland and still want to have a cold treat?"

"It's not a wasteland. It's a desert. Which has its own ecosystem." Forrest playfully poked at Sam's arm as they took their seats across from Charlee and Tina. "And no, ice cream is good all the time and anywhere."

"Hell yeah to that." Tina raised her cup of coffee. "But I feel like we should have ice cream before trivia, just saying."

"Winning team gets first choice." Charlee looked across the room. "And from what I hear there are limited chocolate options, so we are in this to win it."

"Absolutely!" Sam high-fived Charlee.

"So." Charlee pointed her finger at Forrest. "I know you said vanilla is your favorite, but focus. You are my ringer."

Forrest shook his head, "I'm genuinely just here for the company. And ice cream."

"Your favorite ice cream flavor is mint chip." Sam's gaze was hovering on him. "We used to go get it at Joe's Creamery every Friday."

"Not every Friday." Forrest pointed to the front of the canteen. "I think they're getting ready to start."

"Forrest?"

"Is everyone ready to party?" The announcer at the front was one of the kitchen staff. And clearly enjoying the attention turning toward him as everyone in the room shouted "Yes!" in unison.

Sam squeezed his knee. "It's not vanilla."

"Trivia time." Forrest pointed to the announcer, again. He hadn't had ice cream since he walked away from Sam. No trips for cones. No pints at the grocery.

The idea of ice cream had no longer had any appeal after he'd left. So many of the things they'd done together had been off-limits. Packed away memories he never let himself remember.

"What's our team name?" Charlee leaned across the table. "It needs to be good."

"How about Scrub Club?" Sam offered.

"You're the only one that wears scrubs, Doc." Charlee rolled her eyes.

"Not true. Forrest does." Sam nudged him in the ribs with his elbow.

"Only when I'm in the clinic." Forrest ribbed him back. "We are a group of nerds, what about Fellowship of the Quiz."

Charlee made a face.

"I guess not." Forrest laughed. "Any ideas?"

"Dreamhouse Dwellers." Tina giggled. "You know—" she gestured to the bland room "—because this is definitely a dream house and we are all dwelling here for months."

"I think someone is a fan of a certain doll who famously has a dream house." Charlee raised a brow.

Tina shrugged off the comment. "I am. I started collecting them when I was a little girl. We all have our things." She pointed at Charlee. "Your room is covered in troll dolls."

"I have four. That hardly counts as covered." Charlee stuck her tongue out.

"It's a good name." Forrest looked at the announcer who was waiting, not so patiently for the groups to come up with a name. They were hardly the only ones having a hard time with the choice.

"It is." Sam leaned on his hands. "I vote for Dreamhouse Dwellers."

Forrest raised his hand at the same time as Tina and Charlee. "Unanimous."

"I'll go let them know and get our buzzer." Charlee scooted away from the table.

"So we know Charlee likes trolls and I'm into dolls. What hobbies do the two of you have hiding away?"

"I learned to knit and crochet," Sam said. "I have a wild stack of yarn, even used most of my personal allowance of extras bringing yarn with me."

Forrest knew his mouth was hanging open. The fact that Sam was knitting. And crocheting. The man could have said just about anything else and he'd have been less surprised. "Where did you learn to do that?"

"On my rotation in Alaska three years ago. The nights are long and when it was a good night, the hospital was pretty quiet. One of the nurses taught me. It is a great way to keep your mind occupied. Most of my projects go to local shelters. They can always use the hats and socks, whereas I can only have so many pairs before it becomes too much." Sam lifted his pant leg showing of a pair of gray wool socks. "All of the socks I brought were made with my needles."

"That is so cool. My hobby is reading and that seems so unexciting compared to this reveal." Forrest devoured books. Mostly nonfiction and medical journals. As a kid he'd done nothing but borrow mysteries and horror books from the library. Those books were his only escape from the family that on his best days ignored him.

"Not boring." Sam leaned a hand on Forrest's knee as Charlee sat back down.

"Our name is registered and we are going to take this." She set the buzzer in the middle of the table and clapped her hands. "Let's go!"

CHAPTER TWELVE

"I THINK YOUR reading hobby is the only thing that saved us tonight." Sam hit Forrest's hip with his as they started back toward the dorms.

"Who would have guessed that trivia could get so cutthroat?" Forrest raised his hand to a few people walking toward the bar.

Many of the trivia crew had headed that direction when the canteen closed, but Forrest had said he was tired. And Sam had no desire to head to the bar without him.

"Everyone, Forrest." Sam reached for his hand; his body relaxed a little as Forrest's fingers tightened around his. "And then there's the fact that when first chance at a limited selection of ice cream is involved, you apparently *don't* get in Charlee's way."

"That *is* a lesson none of us knew we needed to learn." Forrest chuckled and pulled the door to the dorms open. They stepped inside, knocking the snow off their boots before heading to Sam's room.

It was their nightly ritual. They'd pushed the extra twin bed next to Sam's to create a bigger bed, though they'd woken entwined with each other on one side each morning. Or rather Forrest had woken, kissed Sam and headed out long before the night shifted fully into day.

"That last question, though, was all you." Forrest ran his hand along Sam's shoulder as he unlocked the door to his room.

"Knowing the highest peak in a random US state was certainly lucky. I think Charlee might have lost it if we got that close to first place and then blew it." Sam pushed the door open and pulled Forrest in.

"I've never been to Utah. I've read a few papers from there. And from the pictures I've seen it's gorgeous. Have you spent time there?"

"Not yet." Sam took his boots off and pulled the hat off his head. "But I always do research on potential follow-on locations."

"Utah was on your list before here?" Forrest yawned as he slipped the shirt over his head.

"No. Utah is on the list for after. Utah, back to Alaska again, North Dakota and a few others." Sam had a list in his journal. There was a constant rotation of out of the way places that needed a doctor. Hundreds of places he could go for a few months.

Though the idea of looking at that list didn't hold the same excitement as it had before Forrest had kissed him in the gym. He needed to start planning his next step. His after location, but he couldn't seem to get moving on that agenda item. "Want to shower?"

They were both exhausted. A warm shower would ensure they drifted to sleep faster. And showering with a naked Forrest was never going to be something Sam didn't look forward to.

"The shower is barely big enough for one." Forrest's gaze glowed as he stared at Sam. "I am not complaining but I am exhausted."

Sam stepped up and captured his lips before Forrest could make an excuse for tonight being a cuddle-and-snooze evening. They didn't have to be intimate every night. They had months left together.

"A hot shower, and sleep is the best recipe for exhaustion." Sam pressed his lips to Forrest's rough cheek. "I'll get the water started."

He moved into the bathroom and started the water. "It feels wrong that this place is so cold and the hot water still takes a little while to get going. I feel like the reservoir should be kept nearly boiling so we don't have to shiver for the first seconds." Sam stepped into the cool water and shuddered.

Water rationing wasn't a huge deal in the winter with so few residents. But wasting resources was never recommended.

Forrest stepped in and gave a little shiver as the cool drops hit him. The water started heating and Sam moved to make sure Forrest felt the warmth.

"You ever consider coming to Indianapolis?" Forrest grabbed the soap from the wall and started soaping up the washcloth.

"No." Sam took the washcloth from Forrest and started running it over his back. The muscles were tight. "They have tons of hospitals. Not exactly a rural location."

"That's true." Forrest's head bounced but he didn't add any other comment.

Sam waited a moment, hoping Forrest might ask him to come anyway. Indicate this was more than just an ice fling. Two people drawn together but not meant for forever. But the only sound was the water hitting Forrest's tight back. "Relax." Sam kissed his shoulder. "You'll sleep better if you do."

"Right." Forrest cleared his throat and shifted his shoulders. The relaxation effort didn't seem to work.

"I went hiking in a forest fire once and I don't think my body was this tense." The chuckle that escaped didn't quite cover the fear that still raced through Sam when he remembered the heat that had seemed to radiate from the ground itself.

"What?" Forrest turned; the color drained from his face.

"I went hiking—"

Forrest's hand covered Sam's mouth. "I heard you the first time. Why would you do that?"

Sam took advantage of Forrest's changed position to run the soap over his magnificent chest. "I mean, hiking is fun."

"You know I'm not talking about the damn hike. Or rather I *am*, but seriously, Sam. In a forest fire? That is the definition of reckless." Forrest pursed his lips as he ripped the washcloth from Sam's fingers, added more soap then started running the cloth along Sam's chest.

"Why are you mad? It wasn't intentional. Or, I mean, it was, there were some injured hikers and the fire moved faster than expected. But why are you mad now?" Sam gripped Forrest's cheeks.

"I'm not mad."

"Liar." Sam shook his head but didn't let go of Forrest. "It was years ago. Three assignments ago.

I'm fine." He brushed his lips across Forrest's. "See, fine."

"Have you been anywhere that wasn't dangerous?" Forrest raised a brow but didn't break the connection they had.

"Here." The South Pole was fun. An adventure. Truly unlike any other. "It's pretty safe. But how many people can say they've worked at the South Pole? Maybe I should see about spending time in the North Pole next. Round out the poles."

"There is no permanent station at the North Pole. The ice shifts too much."

"You have so much knowledge up there." Sam pressed his lips to Forrest's temple. The man was gorgeous but his brain was the real turn-on.

"The poles are dangerous." Forrest moved away from Sam's touch to let him into the water.

"Not really." It was a unique place, and there were dangers here. But there were dangers and unpredictability everywhere. Sam had carefully planned out his life twice in "safe" environments and gotten nothing to show for it. Why not explore new locations?

"Sam." Forrest put his hands on Sam's chest. "We are trapped on the pole."

"Evacuations happen. Trapped is a bit of an overstatement."

Drops spun from Forrest's head as he shook his head. "Yes, there has been *an* evacuation."

"Two. I got Dr. Anderson out, too." Sam rinsed quickly then shut the water off. Forrest was hand-ing him a towel before the final drips of the shower head had fallen.

"Anderson got out on the last flight of the season." Forrest wrapped the towel around his waist. "We were lucky to get the two we did. There won't be more. And you know it. So answer the question. Are all the locations you travel to dangerous?"

"Remote work is unique." Sam shrugged as he wrapped the towel around himself.

"Lots of things are unique." Forrest pushed a hand through his damp hair. "Are you seeking out danger?"

"You're here too, Forrest." Sam nodded toward him, then pointed at the phoenix. "Rising from the ashes of what?"

"My life. You said the phoenix made sense. Why are you changing the subject?"

"Because there is no answer to your question." Sam let out a groan of frustration that had nothing to do with the hot, naked man before him.

Or everything to do with him.

"I go where things are interesting. Add memories to my life bank while helping locations with few resources. I stay a couple of months and move on to the next place. I've climbed mountains, helped with fire rescue, damn near died in a plane crash." Sam held up a hand. "Don't tell my mom that. Technically, not a secret but also not something she and Dad know."

"That is the definition of a secret, Sam." Forrest stepped closer to him. "Does Utah have to be next?"

"Nope." Sam shrugged. "It's too soon to think of next. That's a problem for the future. Right now we are on an ice rock. And exhausted." He reached for Forrest's hand and pulled him toward the bed.

"Sam."

He turned, seizing Forrest's mouth. The kiss was deep but didn't linger.

"I do have something to say." Forrest raised a brow. "Not that I mind a kiss but…"

Sam caressed his cheek then laid a finger over his mouth. "Tomorrow."

Forrest let out a sigh.

There were things to talk about. Sam understood that. If they had truly been meant to be, they'd be celebrating a decade of wedded bliss right now and maybe even have a child. But they weren't soulmates.

He'd accepted that years ago. Mostly. This was a respite. This place wasn't real. Forrest had said he didn't know what this thing between them was. Sam wasn't ready to acknowledge the possibility of a future with Forrest stuck in a lab somewhere far from him.

Forrest's arms were around him. His mouth covering Sam's. His hands were stroking his body.

"I thought you were tired." Sam broke the kiss but gripped Forrest's taut ass.

Forrest placed his hands on either side of Sam's cheeks, kissed him and pushed him to the bed.

The questions. The talk. All of it vanished as their bodies tangled together.

* * *

Forrest kissed the end of Sam's nose before slipping from the bed. The alarm on his wrist started buzzing as he pulled on his pants and grabbed a shirt. He'd woken up just before it went off. So his body was already starting to adjust.

He'd gotten about three hours of sleep. Less than ideal, but he'd make it work.

He quietly opened the door and slipped out, careful not to wake Sam.

He blinked as the lights of the hallway hit his eyes. His brain rebelled and he sucked in a deep breath. He did not have time to get a migraine. There were two experiments to check on today. He had to gather the samples people had dropped off. Swab them to see what was growing. And put together some reports for his team back stateside. Then he'd stop by the clinic.

He yawned as he made his way to his room. Not that he'd slept there in the last week.

A week.

That was all the time that had passed since they spent the first night together. So there was no reason for Sam to indicate he was thinking of uprooting the life he had for a future together.

He has no roots.

Forrest pushed past that thought as he hastily picked out clothes for the day. He grabbed some pain reliever, hoping that, if he got ahead of the headache, it might stay just a headache.

Trudging through the snow to the first pickup location, he nearly slipped on the ice. "Not dangerous, my ass."

He bit his lip. There was no need to talk to himself and Sam was clearly more of an adrenaline junkie than he'd been in school.

He wasn't one.

Except this didn't feel like he was chasing a rush. Sam was still in control. Still choosing his locations. He was in control; it was just instead of planning decades into the future he was only focused on the next twelve months or so.

Forrest wanted to look further. He'd wanted to talk about Indianapolis. Wanted to bring up the possibility of forever. Wanted to talk about this thing between them working.

Years of therapy had helped him identify the trauma of his youth. Helped him acknowledge that abuse. He wasn't petrified of the altar and letting a spouse down—though he hadn't properly dated anyone to test that theory.

Because all he'd wanted was Sam.

Something he'd wanted to say last night. But something in Sam's look had silenced him.

Had made him fear that Sam might walk away now. Might say this was simply one of the fun things he tried out when he was someplace new. After all, there wasn't a ton to do on the ice.

Forrest pressed a thumb to his temple. The pressure point sometimes relieved a bit of the force in his skull. Today it gained him nothing as he opened the door to a building where he'd set up a sample collection. He needed to move fast.

He grabbed the first samples and headed to the second location, blinking as an aura appeared in the corner of his eye.

He didn't bother to muffle the curse. He was on borrowed time. An hour. Maybe two. And he had at least six hours of solid work in front of him. Which meant working through the pain.

Picking up the pace he raced through collections and headed to the lab.

"Damn." Charlee lifted her head from the mat she'd laid on the floor. "Seriously? Seriously?" She slowly stood, groaning with each movement as she headed to the wall.

Forrest flinched as she flicked on a light. "What are you doing here?" Charlee didn't show up until nine. She worked late and slept in. If you counted sleeping until seven as sleeping in.

"What are *you* doing here?" Charlee crossed her arms. "I suspected you were here before six, but Forrest it is three thirty."

Forrest walked over and flicked the light off. His brain couldn't handle it. "Couldn't sleep."

"I don't believe that." Charlee reached for the light again.

"Don't, please."

Her hand paused as she looked him over. "I spent the night here to test my theory and I *hate* that I was right. You need to get more rest."

"I'm fine, Charlee. This isn't the first time my

body has operated on little rest. Just settling it back into the rhythm it kept through my teens and twenties." Forrest couldn't manage to catch the yawn and saw Charlee's frown in the dimly lit lab.

"Go to bed, Charlee." There was no need to for her to be anything other than rested.

"Go back to bed, Forrest." Charlee imitated the frustration in his voice.

"I am already up and once that happens there is no point." Plus he needed to get this done before the migraine fully sidelined him.

"This is a bad idea. I'm telling you that right now." Charlee pointed a finger at him then yawned.

He couldn't stop the yawn that mimicked hers.

"I'm too tired to argue. But we *are* talking about this when I'm awake enough to make a solid argument." Charlee walked out, but at least she didn't slam the door.

Forrest took care of the samples, doing his best to ignore the growing aura in his left eye. There was no use ignoring the pounding in his head. That he was just going to have to deal with.

After getting the samples put away, he started toward the experiments he was monitoring. His brain screamed and he closed his eyes, sucking air through his teeth. If he gave it a moment, something would give.

It had to.

He shifted his shoulders and pushed at the darkness that seemed to pull at the edges of his senses.

Then he opened his eyes, waiting for the sensation to cease. But it closed in tighter, tighter and then...

"Forrest."

Soft hands cupped his face. Sam's hands. The dream felt so real. Forrest tried to lift his arm to search out the man behind the hands, but his dream body was so heavy.

"Forrest. I need you to open your eyes."

Such a demand. Forrest tried to summon the energy but again his dream body refused.

"Now! Forrest." Charlee's voice echoed on the edge of his mind.

Weird. He never dreamed of colleagues, but the subconscious was peculiar.

"Call the clinic. Tell them to get a bed ready." Sam's voice sounded just like it had on their first rotation in med school. Sure, but a little afraid. "And a gurney. I doubt he can move on his own right now."

"Sam." His tongue was too large. And the headache he'd had was roaring back. This wasn't a dream, or it was too real. Either way it wasn't fair that his head now ached more than before. "Sam?"

"Forrest. Open your eyes."

He shook his head and flinched as the movement sent pain rushing toward him. "Lights off. Please."

"What the hell is that supposed to mean?" Charlee moved in the distance.

"It means a migraine. Move your right hand, if that is true."

Forrest did as he was told. His whole head felt like it might explode. "Aura started an hour ago."

"No. It didn't. It's eight a.m. You've been on the ground for, I don't even want to guess how long." Sam's clipped tone reached into his soul.

"You okay?" Forrest reached out a hand, trying to find Sam's by the sound of his voice.

"No. My boyfriend has been on the floor of his lab for hours. He cut the back of head when he fell and is suffering a migraine so bad, he can't even sit up. And I'm guessing there were hints of the headache when you slipped out of bed this morning."

Boyfriend.

Forrest thought he was smiling as the word punctured his skull.

"Thought I could work through it."

"Uh-huh." Sam's voice was rough with emotion, "Chris, let's get him loaded."

"I can walk." The idea of being brought into the clinic on a gurney made his stomach turn. Or maybe that was just the migraine.

"All evidence points to that *not* being the case." Charlee's voice was level but he heard the hint of fear, too. He must look terrible.

"Thank you, Charlee." Sam put his hands on Forrest's cheeks just like they'd been when he thought he was dreaming. It settled him.

"If you can open your eyes right now, without flinching, and stand. Then I will walk you to the clinic." Sam's pulled back. The heat his touch provided evaporated and Forrest tried to ignore the chill sliding down his body.

He swallowed and opened his eyes. The dim lights turned his stomach and he rolled. There was a bucket before him to take care of the issue. Thank goodness.

"I think that covers it." Sam put his arms under Forrest's body and hefted him onto the gurney while Chris strapped him down.

Forrest couldn't even work up the energy to say something as the darkness pressed against him again. This time he didn't try to hold it off.

CHAPTER THIRTEEN

THERE WAS AN IV in his arm. That was what Forrest noticed before the fact that his headache was now a dull ache. A migraine cocktail must be pumping into his system.

He'd never gotten one before but had ordered several during his tenure in the ER during residency. It was an IV with fluids, nausea meds and pain meds. He'd seen more than one person begging for the cocktail over less effective, treatments. As a migraine sufferer, Forrest had never hesitated to start the drugs right away.

"Finally understand why these things are rated so highly on exit surveys."

"What?"

Forrest opened his eyes and smiled as Sam lifted his head off the bed. "I didn't mean to say that out loud."

"Clearly." Sam stood and rolled his shoulders. "I take it that means the cocktail worked?"

"Yeah. Once it's finished, I need—"

"No. You don't," Sam interrupted.

Forrest's head snapped, and the drugs had clearly worked because he wasn't ready to toss the very limited contents of his stomach again. "You don't even know what I was about to say."

"You're right." Sam crossed his arms. "I'm not sure if you're going to say that you need to get back to the lab or to help out here. Either way, I know for a fact that you're going to say that you need to head to work." He lifted his chin, the dare clear in his eyes.

"I was actually going to see about finding food." That was a lie and it was clear from the twitch in Sam's cheek that he knew it.

"Good. I have food here. That's easy enough to fix." Sam walked out of the bay.

Why the hell was he so upset? Forrest was the one in the bed.

Boyfriend.

The word echoed in his brain. Sam had said that when his voice was raised in the lab. Hadn't he? Forrest was more than a little foggy on the details.

Sam walked back in with a standard issue hospital tray.

Forrest shuddered. "That isn't just gelatin, is it?" The joke fell flat.

"It's dinner from the canteen. Charlee made you a to-go plate from the buffet. She even managed to squeeze in some ice cream. Not vanilla." Sam set the tray down.

"Dinner? Wait. What time is it?" How long had he been out?

"It's almost six a.m."

6:00 a.m.? Six in the morning? Forrest sat up further in the bed. He'd lost an entire day. An entire day.

No. He was already so far behind. This wasn't happening.

"Who took my shift?"

"That is your question?" Sam took the chair by the bed and laid a hand on Forrest's knee.

"Yeah. The first of a few actually. The sample collection..."

"You passed out from a migraine after sneaking from bed at three yesterday morning."

"I didn't sneak. I kissed your nose and I left, and it wasn't three." Forrest cleared his throat. There was no need to add that last part. This wasn't an interrogation.

Or rather it was, but he was not required to give the whole truth and nothing but the truth.

"So sorry, two forty-five? Is that closer?"

It was, but there was no reason to go down that route. "Sam, I'm fine."

Sam pursed his lips before letting out a breath. There were dark circles under his eyes and his lips looked chapped. When they'd dated, he had a bad habit of rubbing them until they bled.

He's worried about me.

Forrest understood. If the roles were reversed, he'd be terrified.

"I am fine." Forrest repeated the words. "I've suffered from migraines for as long as I can remember. They come when I am stressed." He was just exhausted from trying to meet all the expectations. He hadn't felt like he was covering so many spinning plates since med school. But he didn't want to let Sam down. The man would push himself to the brink in an instant.

Combine all that with the questions constantly popping off in Forrest's brain about the state of his and Sam's relationship, and it was stunning the migraine hadn't appeared days ago.

"I know." Sam stood, rubbed a finger along his bottom lip. "I know they come when you're stressed. You're doing too much. You're in the clinic, but the lab work is still there." He took a deep breath. "You aren't superman. I think we need to prioritize one of them."

Forrest's brain was still mushy. There wasn't a priority. He belonged in the lab, but he was helping in the clinic. Needed in the clinic—at least for now. "Says the man who never came to get me as backup when half the post was down with a bug." Forrest knew it was petulant to bring that up. But he was not the only overachieving burnt-out physician in this small bay.

"That was different." Sam moved to the end of the bed and leaned his hands on the rails. "You were busy."

"And you were drowning in patients. You were convinced you could handle it on your own."

"I could have." Sam bent his head. "But I'm glad that I didn't need to. And you don't need to do this, either." He waved a hand toward the bed. "I talked to Charlee."

"Charlee is not running the same experiments as I am." Not exactly a lie. Charlee and he were on the same team, but the microbiologist was looking for bacterial growth while he was focusing on shifting viral loads and when mutations occurred.

"You ran the lab when she was down with the

virus that took out so many here. And you have free time. She pointed that out while you were sleeping." Sam leaned farther over the railing. "You need to rest. Doctor's orders. I will confine you to the barracks."

"No, you won't." Forrest shook his head. "No. You won't. You need me here. You need another physician of record. I can get everything done." He'd done it for most of his life. "I am not failing at this."

"Do you hear yourself? You didn't fail. You passed the eff out!" Sam leaned back and crossed his arms. "I am rotating you back to two shifts in here. And I will check in with Charlee to make sure that you are only working ten-hour days." He turned on his heel.

"Sam." At least that stopped him from walking out. "Don't leave." The plea was so quiet, Forrest wasn't completely sure he'd said it.

Sam's shoulder's tightened, but he stayed where he was, though he didn't look back. "I need to grab the tablet and update your chart. I will be right back. Eat your dinner. Please, Forrest."

Then he opened the bay curtain and stepped out.

Sam shuddered as the wave of emotions wrapped around him. The last twenty-four hours had been a roller coaster. He'd panicked when Charlee called. Felt his heart stop when he'd seen Forrest on the floor of the lab. And now he was angry the man was trying to do everything.

Because I keep putting him on the roster.

And then there was the guilt. Sam had added more shifts than he needed. It had been a selfish play to spend more time with Forrest. To re-create the magic they'd had in med school and help Forrest stop hiding away, wasting his talents.

All I did was drive him to a migraine.

"He isn't wrong." Nat held the tablet close to her chest as Sam walked up to the desk. "You're just as bad. You've been better since he's been on the rotation, but you're two peas in the same pod."

Sam didn't have a comment ready to fire off for that one, so he just held his hand out for the tablet.

Natasha shook her head. "You aren't allowed to be the medical person of record for your boyfriend. You know the rules."

"We aren't boyfriends." Sam's throat threatened to close as he whispered the words.

"Really?" She raised a brow and grabbed the walkie-talkie. "Should I check with Charlee to find out if she fully misheard you while you were trying to rouse the man that anyone can see is definitely not not your boyfriend this morning?"

Sam did not appreciate the double negative. Or the reminder that he'd called Forrest his boyfriend. Seeing him on the ground, the blood on the back of his head… It had taken all of Sam's training to keep his breath steady and focus on providing care.

Even now, his fingers were shaking at the idea that Forrest had lain on that cold floor for hours before Charlee found him. The cut on the back of his head hadn't needed stitches. A butterfly bandage was enough to close the wound that had mostly stopped bleeding by the time they got him to the hospital. But what if it hadn't been enough?

If he'd lain there, bleeding. Hurt. Alone.

He didn't.

"Fine." He wasn't going to argue semantics with Natasha, or Charlee for that matter. Forrest hadn't heard him. They weren't boyfriends. Not anymore.

But that didn't mean Sam's soul hadn't cracked for a moment when he saw him.

"You need to rest." Nat punched a few things on the tablet.

"I've slept."

"Oh. You are testy." She set the tablet down and crossed her arms. "I said *rest*. Not sleep. Sleep is important. It resets our cycles and helps our bodies regulate. But that's not what I meant. And you know it. Do you know how to rest?"

"Of course." Sam knew how to rest. He just wasn't very good at it. His body seemed to rebel at the idea of just sitting still. Of letting time pass without accomplishing anything. Every person got a finite amount of time on this planet, and he craved movement. Slowing down gave your brain time to think. Time to question.

"Really?" Natasha chuckled. "What did you bring as your personal item?"

He could tell from the look in her eyes that she didn't expect him to have anything. Sam raised his chin. "Yarn. Knitting needles and crochet hooks."

Her brows furrowed as she stepped around the desk, heading for Forrest's bay.

"No comment? I am pretty sure you expected me to say I didn't need a personal item." Natasha was a lot of things, but the woman did not let go of a point she was making.

Pushing the curtain back on, Nat smiled at the man picking through the food on the plate. "What was your personal item?"

"What?" Forrest looked from Natasha to Sam.

"I said, what was your personal item? The thing that didn't count against you on the weight allowance for personal belongings—within reason. We all got something we were allowed to bring provided it wasn't a weapon. And somehow, Forrest, you don't strike me as a big game hunter or shooter."

"I'm not. I brought my guitar." His dark gaze flitted to Sam before focusing back on his food.

He'd mentioned the guitar during one of their first conversations. But Sam had never seen it in his room. Was it the one he'd given him? The one he'd picked at on their old comfy blue couch for years. If Sam closed his eyes, he could place Forrest there now. Rerun a memory he hadn't thought of in ages.

Forrest had joked for a year that he'd love to learn play. For Christmas, Sam had put it under the tree, unsurprised when Forrest let out an excited squeal upon seeing it. Christmas—the holiday he loved most even though his family never celebrated it or gave him a gift. Sam had always tried to make it special, but he'd never topped that guitar.

Forrest had spent all his free time watching online videos and taking online music lessons since his schedule couldn't accommodate in-person lessons easily.

He had loved that instrument. And the apartment had been so silent after he'd left. The ghosts of music Sam would never hear again had echoed in his memories long after Forrest disappeared from his life.

"Great. A guitar and fiber arts." Natasha grabbed a prescription pad from her pocket.

"Are you planning on ordering me to knit?" Sam chuckled but Natasha didn't look up as she scribbled one note, ripped it off and scribbled another.

"No." She pressed one note into his chest and dropped the other on the tray next to the food Forrest was barely touching. "I'm ordering you *both* to knit and play the guitar. You are not to return to this clinic for the next three days." She held up a hand toward Forrest. "Or the lab."

"Hey." The fact that Forrest's complaint was so loud was a good thing. It meant the migraine cocktail had worked. Though Natasha was right, he still needed to take some time off.

"I have Charlee monitoring the lab." Nat interrupted Forrest before his "Hey" could become more than a single ticked-off statement. "Do not make that woman mad. And you—" she turned her full attention to Sam "—do *not* try me. I will not have you back in this clinic for three days. Attempt it, and I will talk to Houston."

There was very little Houston could do. There was no way off the ice right now. But the look on Nat's face was enough to give Sam at least second thoughts about trying her.

"I'll take a day." That would be good because then he could make sure that Forrest relaxed.

"I am sorry, Doc, did I order a day?" She looked over at Forrest who shook his head.

"I think it was three."

Sam raised a brow as the man he'd spent every night with for a week sided with the NP.

"You're planning to make me take three days." Forrest crossed his arms.

"*You* were on the floor of your lab bleeding this morning. I have no such issue."

"Yet."

"Yet."

Natasha and Forrest's voices echoed into the clinic at the same time.

"I will be checking in." He was the resident physician. It was his job.

"So you don't think Chris and I are capable. That's a tough hit, but I'm not surprised." Natasha pulled back, her shoulders tight.

"That's not what I said." Sam pushed a hand through his hair. He could see how the words could be taken that way. But it wasn't what he'd meant.

"Take the time, Sam." Forrest's words were strong. Something Sam would be celebrating after the day's escapades. If they weren't directed at keeping him out of the clinic.

"Listen to him." Natasha walked over and started to pull the IV out of Forrest's arm. "I'm discharging you. I'm sending along some pain meds that you are to take if you start to feel any headache or see any aura."

"I don't usually see the aura, and never without the migraine." Forrest held the bandage over the small puncture wound and placed his hand over his head to help with clotting.

"There's a first time for everything." Natasha pulled the gloves off, walked out and was back in no time with the pain meds she'd promised. "Walk him back to the dorms, Doc."

Then she turned on her heel.

"That is one tough nurse." Forrest slid his feet over the edge of the bed and into the boots Sam had removed when they'd brought him in. "I don't think I'd want to go up against her."

Sam tilted his head. "Really?"

Forrest mirrored his head tilt. "Really."

"I'll take some time off." It wasn't going to be three days. But he could take two. Make sure Forrest was fully recovered. "Let's go. Slowly." He slid his arm around Forrest's waist.

Forrest leaned against him. "I'm fine."

Sam's mind knew that, but it was having a hard time convincing his heart.

CHAPTER FOURTEEN

Forrest rolled over on the bed and let out a moan. He wasn't sure what time it was. His head was delightfully pain-free, but his muscles were clearly upset by the lack of movement.

Lifting his wrist, he blinked as bare skin stared back. "What?" He lifted the other, not that he ever wore his watch on his right wrist, but it was also bare.

"If you are looking for your watch, it's sitting on the counter by the door. Damn thing went off at two forty-five this morning. I should have made sure you turned the alarm off." Sam looked up from the couch where he was knitting a sock.

"Sorry." Forrest had meant to turn it off.

"Were you planning to disregard Nat's orders?" Sam's hands kept moving as he looked directly at Forrest. There were creases around his eyes and dark circles indicating that while Forrest was well rested, Sam couldn't say the same.

"How are you doing that?" Forrest asked. Sam's hands were flying but he wasn't looking at the sock.

"Don't change the subject." The needles he was holding kept the same pace even though he never looked down.

"I'm not. Not really." Forrest slid out of bed and started to stretch. After so many hours in bed yesterday and then oversleeping, his body felt refreshed but tight. "I meant to turn it off. The headache. The day. It must have slipped my mind. It's habit that it goes off so early."

Sam let out a noise that made Forrest think there was more than a little bit of doubt in his mind. "Habit. You mean to tell me that you've been getting up that early for years?"

"No. I shifted after Dr. Anderson left." Not completely truthful. And the lie rubbed his soul. "I shifted after the virus. I was working in the lab and the clinic."

"Then it is not habit." Sam blew out a breath as his needles flew even faster through the stitches.

"You're mad."

The knitting needles clicked together and now Sam did look down.

"Because I got you banished from the hospital for three days?" Forrest pursed his lips. The man belonged in the clinic. In trauma centers. Sam was born to be a doctor. Forrest had fallen into it because he was good at school. A school counselor recommended it and he'd followed the path. But Sam—Sam was meant to heal.

But burnout didn't care about your passions or callings. It struck everyone. And Sam was hovering on the precipice of it. Or already covering it up and trying to deny it.

The needles' clicking stopped. "No. Yes. Not entirely." Sam exhaled heavily. "You were passed out."

"The migraine—"

"Forrest." Sam pinched his eyes closed. "You were passed out on the lab floor for hours. What if you'd hit your head harder? What if the scrape on the back of your head was a gash? What if the migraine was the warning of an aneurysm?" When he opened his eyes, they were full of fire.

There was no way Forrest was going to point out that, if his headache was the rare sign of an aneurysm, there was nothing that could be done at the pole. Sam's hands were already shaking.

Forrest moved to the couch. He reached for the knitting, but Sam pulled back.

"I am furious with you." He swallowed. "And with myself for not catching it. I knew you were sneaking out. Knew you were putting too much pressure on yourself. Knew I wasn't helping with that."

"I was not sneaking—stop saying that. That makes it sound like I was doing something wrong." He'd been trying to keep everything going. Trying to ensure everything got done. Trying to make sure nothing failed. He didn't fail.

In the end he hadn't been able to accomplish it. And gotten Sam banished from the hospital for his efforts, too. "And you weren't making me do anything I wasn't fully on board with."

Sam shuddered. "You could have been seriously hurt, Forrest." His words echoed off the walls of the room and color shot up his cheeks as he realized how loud he was.

"But I wasn't." Forrest laid his hand on Sam's knee. "I am fine."

"How would you feel if it was me?" Sam sucked in a breath as his jeweled gaze captured Forrest's.

Forrest swallowed as he found no words on the edge of his tongue. If he'd walked in on Sam passed out, he'd have panicked. From the account Charlee had told him, Sam had flown into physician mode. Taken charge and never wavered.

"I'd have panicked."

"No." Sam shook his head. "You wouldn't have. That's a fiction that you are telling yourself because you're convinced you're not good at bedside. But I didn't ask what you would do. I asked how you'd *feel* if it was me."

"Broken." The words slipped from his lips. That was his heart answering.

"I asked you before this—" Sam gestured between the two of them "—started, what we are doing. You didn't answer. We still haven't addressed any of it. We slid right back into the day to day and nights." Color climbed Sam's throat. "I found you on the floor unconscious."

"And called me your boyfriend." Forrest was certain he'd heard that.

Nearly certain.

"Forrest—" Sam set the yarn to the side "—I said it out of habit."

Knives slicing through him. Each word a blade cutting deeper.

Habit. That wasn't what he wanted to be. Wasn't what he needed. But he also had never broached the topic of their relationship. "Habit." Forrest pursed his lips. "Is that what I am? A habit?"

Sam let out a breath, "I mean the word *boyfriend*

slipped out because you were my boyfriend for so long. I've avoided asking, Forrest, because I'm terrified that you will just say you don't know what this is between us. You walked away once before. It destroyed me."

"It wasn't supposed to." He bit his tongue. "I didn't mean to say that."

Sam nodded. "Didn't mean to say it but meant it. Right?"

What was the point of denying it? "Yes. You aren't supposed to be here, Sam." Forrest laughed but there was no hint of humor in it. Sam was meant for so much more. "You're supposed to be in New York running a trauma unit. Visiting your parents upstate on the weekends with your husband."

"I don't believe in marriage." Sam cleared his throat.

"You believed once upon a time. Planned it all out." Forrest's neck twitched as he caught himself from looking at the door. Escape was cowardly. And Sam was right. He'd asked twice and Forrest had dodged the question.

Sam shrugged. "Not anymore. I deserve to know, need to know, what the hell this is. Because putting myself back together again was the hardest thing I've ever done. So one final ask, what are we doing?"

"I never stopped loving you, Sam." Forrest met the blue eyes that had haunted him for so long. "Never. And if you had been on the floor of the hospital unconscious, my soul would have torn apart. And yes, I would have slipped into doctor mode.

Because a world without you is less bright. I know that. I lived it."

"Because you chose it." Sam's bottom lip trembled, but his shoulders straightened. "I thought this was just a fun ice fling. A moment suspended in time."

That stung. But Forrest had never indicated that it was anything else. He'd forced himself back into Sam's life. Literally. Sam was right. He'd asked, more than once, what they were doing.

It was Forrest holding back. Forrest terrified of giving the wrong answer. But no answer was also an answer. Sam deserved more.

"I don't want this to be an ice fling." This was a fork in the road. Once this conversation finished there was no going back.

"Then what *do* you want, Forrest?"

So few people had ever asked him that. In fact the first person to ever ask was the man sitting across from him. The man whose heart he'd crave for the rest of his days. "You. Always, you."

Sam nodded but didn't say anything. Silence stretched into the moment. Heavy with the past, present and hopefully future.

When he still didn't say anything, Forrest pulled back a little. "Do you want me to leave?" Sam had asked the question. Forrest had given the answer. If it wasn't what Sam wanted, needed, Forrest would honor that.

"I don't want you to leave." Sam closed the distance between them but didn't reach for him. Didn't touch him. "If this isn't an ice fling…"

"It isn't." Forrest should have let him finish his sentence but he needed to acknowledge that now. This was not a fling. Not for him.

"Then we are boyfriends. Lovers. Whatever label the world puts on it." Sam sighed.

"What label do you want?" Forrest was fine with anything, provided the other person in the relationship was Sam.

"Boyfriends feels like we are back in college. In that one-bedroom apartment with no insulation between our walls." Sam chuckled, the mood lightening. "But lovers feels… I don't know not wrong but not right. Partners is too—" he paused for a second "—serious at the moment."

Forrest put his hand on Sam's chin, "If people ask, we can say boyfriends, but honestly, outside of Natasha and Charlee, who have both made their thoughts very clear, I don't think anyone else is paying attention. And I mean that in the best way. So for us, we are simply Forrest and Sam. Two men who don't want to be separated. Does that work?"

Sam nodded. "Yeah. That works."

Forrest leaned in. His lips brushed Sam's. A kiss to seal the moment. In many ways it was anticlimactic. But it was also perfection. They were Forrest and Sam again.

And this time, Forrest wasn't walking away. "Now, how about you teach me how to crochet? Not sure I can do two hooks."

"These are needles." Sam winked before standing and walking over to a bag and coming back.

"This—" he held up a small blue device "—is a hook." He grabbed some yellow yarn out of the bag.

"I know that is yarn."

"Good." Sam dropped a kiss on his nose. "Let's get started."

It wasn't until they were in bed that evening that Forrest realized he'd said he loved Sam. Sam had said he didn't want him to leave. That he didn't want a fling. But he'd never said the word *love*.

"We should go get your guitar." Sam stretched and rolled his shoulders.

"Bored?"

"Yes!" He was not going to lie about that. This was day three of Natasha's mandated free time. But the problem with free time was that it made time pass so slowly.

"You've been so many places, Sam. Surely you didn't work *all* the time at them. You said you investigated locations before going, no point in that if you are only planning to be in the clinic."

"I did stuff." Touristy things mostly. Things to fill the space between shifts. But he hadn't gone more than twenty-four hours between shifts in years. It was one of Oliver's primary complaints.

Stop working so hard. Have some free time.

Cheating was never the answer, but Sam would only be lying to himself if he didn't acknowledge that he'd prioritized work over that relationship. Another piece of proof that, when the universe crafted him, he wasn't cut out for the type of soulmate love his parents had.

I told Forrest this wasn't a fling.

Sam still wasn't sure how to wrangle the mixed emotions in his soul. One part of him had wanted to explode with joy. Send a note back to his parents announcing that they were back together. That they could expect to see them when they got back.

But a thread of fear still roamed his heart. He'd been so sure once. Believed that Forrest was the "one." That he *had* a one. Then Forrest had walked away. Sam had never guessed he was even considering it. He'd spent months going over their time together, looking for the red flags people said must be there.

Only to find none.

So this wasn't a fling, but he was going to monitor the situation this time. Make sure he saw any changes. Had time to react. Protect himself.

Flee.

"So we could do stuff here. There are activities." Forrest walked over to the bulletin board right before the door and grabbed the weekly activity list that was pushed under the door each Monday. Sam always hung it up, but other than trivia night he'd never done anything on it.

"There is a lecture, but it isn't until this evening." Forrest pulled his bottom lip through his teeth.

"And nothing else for the day, right? This place isn't a tourist destination." Sam fought the urge to walk to the clinic, just to check in. If he did that, he'd never hear the end of it from Natasha.

And if he was honest, he was a little terrified of the NP. Which he knew was the image she cultivated—well.

"What was your favorite thing you've done? Ice fishing? You were up north."

Sam laughed. "Up north yes, I've been above the lower forty-eight, as the Alaskans call it. But no ice fishing. The weather was far too cold for my liking. Plus sitting on the ice for hours was not exactly enticing for me. There are other activities in Alaska besides ice-related ones. Not so much the case here."

"When we get ice storms in Indianapolis it shuts the city completely down." Forrest pulled one arm across his chest then the other. "But it doesn't happen often. Not even every year."

"Uh-huh." Forrest had brought up his hometown several times over the last two days but never asked him to come. "Shutting down for ice is the case in most places I am pretty sure." Sam winked, enjoying the face Forrest made,

"The *point*, Sam, is what did you do? You said you enjoyed being in new places. What did you enjoy?"

"Moving." Sam shrugged. "I know moving is something most people hate, but I enjoyed it. I liked throwing darts, sort of, and landing someplace I never knew existed. I have a goal to visit all fifty states and as many countries as possible."

A goal he only accomplished through work, but he was accomplishing it.

"So travel." Forrest blew out a breath. "Not really an option at the pole, or with only one more day off. But, where do you want to go next? We can plan it."

Plan it. Sam's stomach clenched. Plan. With Forrest. It was a lovely suggestion. One he wanted. So why was his voice suddenly absent?

Forrest looked down and grabbed a shirt that had escaped the laundry bag he kept at the end of the bed. Hiding the disappointment Sam's hesitation no doubt brought. "Or we could do laundry. It's time."

Saying the words in a dramatic fashion did not make that chore any more exciting.

"It is. But we should find something to entertain us while the machine runs. And I think you've knotted enough yarn for today." Sam picked up the ball of yellow that Forrest had managed to mangle. "How is this even possible?"

Forrest looked at the ball of yarn, but Sam doubted the frustration darting through his features had anything to do with the yarn. Why hadn't he said something about planning a trip?

Made a plan. That was what Sam was good at. Plan out the next six months. Do something. But the words refused to materialize.

"We can grab my guitar and spend time in the lounge while we wait for it. Weird how domestic duties are still required at the end of the earth."

"Let's grab the guitar." Sam was surprised how much he wanted to see the instrument in Forrest's large hands. It had always struck him how gently he cradled the instrument, how those fingers were so deft on the strings. Ironic considering the complete lack of dexterity with the crochet hook. "Then we can do what needs to be done with these."

Forrest grabbed the laundry bag that filled twice as fast with two men's clothes. Sam should be grateful that he wasn't pushing the conversation about planning a vacation. So why was he annoyed that Forrest had shifted to laundry—the most boring chore—so fast? If Forrest didn't force the issue, what did that mean?

They got to Forrest's room; Forrest opened the door and stepped inside. He went to the small closet and pulled out a hard case. Not the case Sam had gotten him.

"You changed cases?" Sam pointed at the plain black case. It was functional but lacked the fun vibrancy of the red Sam had purchased for it.

"No. This guitar came with this case. I thought of adding stickers to it. Or something to change it up, but I rarely use it, so no real point." Forrest put the guitar over his shoulder.

"What happened to the one I gave you?" The question was out before Sam could capture it. He'd kept the watch Sam had given him. The one that had brought so many emotions.

But the watch was functional. Something that had use. An instrument was useful, but the guitar was a deeper gift. A thing Forrest had always wanted but would never buy for himself. If he'd given it away... Sam swallowed.

Forrest's hand stopped as he reached for the laundry basket. He looked up and stepped toward Sam.

Sam's face must be showing the turmoil wrapping through his soul.

Forrest held up a hand. "It's at home. In the corner of my apartment that my friend Kelly is house sitting until I get back. There was no way I was bringing my prize possession to the end of the earth. It's the one thing I have that is irreplaceable. Well, that and the Christmas ornaments I've kept in a box in my closet."

Most of the heaviness, the worry, the fear coating Sam's heart melted on that statement. He closed the distance between the two of them. His mouth covering Forrest's as he wrapped his arms around his neck.

He loved this man. Had always loved this man. Sam broke the connection and put his hands on either side of Forrest's face. The stubble that Forrest perpetually left on his jaw now sharp under his fingers.

I love you.

The words were sharp in his mind. Crystal clear. But his mouth couldn't quite form the words. His brain was still firing off what-ifs that served no purpose.

"I missed those clay figures on the tree." Sam pressed his forehead to Forrest's. He'd always given him such a hard time when he sought out the yearly ornaments at the small stand that popped up right after Halloween and disappeared the day after Christmas. For Forrest it was a pilgrimage.

He'd missed everything about this man. If they made it to the end of the year, they were going to have to get a new ornament.

When, his heart reminded his brain, not if. When.

CHAPTER FIFTEEN

Natasha leaned back in the chair at the desk. "I got an offer to work in Florida."

Sam looked up from notes he was making. "Oh. I didn't know you were looking to go to Florida." Time on the ice was winding down.

Nat shrugged. "Gotta have a follow-on location."

Sam made a noncommittal sound. He and Forrest were doing great. The last few weeks had been nearly perfect. It was like before. Nearly.

Yet anytime Forrest brought up Indianapolis or even a vacation after this, Sam always found a way to change the subject. It wasn't that he didn't like the idea of Indianapolis. He'd never put it on his list, but that was because it wasn't on any list he'd seen.

Even if he wasn't ready to discuss moving in, a vacation after working pretty much nonstop on the ice for eight months was a great idea. And it had been a perfect month and a half. So he should help Forrest pick a place.

But something kept holding him back. His brain refused to listen to his heart. Refused to accept that this time maybe everything would be fine. If it hadn't worked last time, what was the guarantee it would work this time?

"I mean, I'm not sure that I want to go to Florida, but as a traveler it's a decent location. And after here—" she gestured to the ice-coated window "—warm sounds good."

Sam laughed. "That I understand."

"Where are you headed? Indiana?"

"Did Forrest put you up to asking that?" Sam feared the question sounded as pathetic as it felt.

"Of course not. But I know that's where the lab is based. Charlee and I are already planning to meet up for girls' night in the city when a big music tour comes through next year."

The two women had become fast friends after concocting a plan to force Forrest and Sam to take time off. It was weird that was over a month ago. He'd expected the time to drag here. Instead it was speeding by.

Sam knew that Forrest would be getting similar questions from Charlee. No secrets between the lab and the clinic.

"So where are you planning to go?"

The door to the hospital opened at the same time as that question left Natasha's lips and Forrest walked in. They'd started splitting shifts. Chris, Natasha, and Sam all working overlapping tens with Forrest subbing in six in the afternoon.

"Scrap that question." Natasha passed the tablet to Forrest.

"I didn't mean to interrupt. But I was sick of hiding in the lab. The tests are just spinning."

Hiding in the lab.

There was that language he'd used the entire time he was here. Yet, he didn't show any interest in changing it. Why?

And if he wasn't happy in the lab, would he uproot

and change everything like he had in med school? And would Sam be the casualty when it happened again?

"You didn't." Natasha stretched an arm over her shoulder. "But I'm off and I'm not wasting an extra minute here. You two—" she pointed at both of them "—should do the same."

"We do." Sam shook his head as Natasha darted toward the door. "Most of the time."

"When things aren't busy." Forrest nodded along with him and let out a laugh. "We aren't working ourselves to the bone right now."

"I think Natasha would point out that the words *right now* make that comment suspicious." Sam slapped Forrest on the back. If they weren't at the clinic he'd kiss him, but that would have to wait until his shift ended.

"Then it's a good thing she didn't hear it and my boyfriend has no desire to inform her." Forrest hit his hip as he looked at the bays. "How has today been?"

"Steady." Sam had seen a handful of patients. Nothing requiring an overnight stay. "It's a little weird."

"What?" Forrest headed to the chair behind the desk to take a quick look at the day's charts. Even with no patients at the moment, he always familiarized himself with the day's load.

He noticed patterns before anyone else. Like the fact that there was a pinpoint carbon monoxide leak in one of the dorms. Three people on the same end of one hall had reported headaches when they were talking at dinner three nights ago. Each mentioned how they woke up with the headaches but they went away a few hours after work. The carbon monoxide detector would have caught it, after it got bigger, but Forrest had found it immediately.

"I don't want to say the Q-word." Sam looked at the door as if just thinking the word *quiet* was enough to bring a rush of patients.

Forrest put his hands on the desk. "It is a unique environment. Everyone is healthy. The kind of chronic diseases we see on the mainland don't exist here."

We. Sam's heart thudded in his ears. Forrest had started talking about himself as one of the doctors. Not a stand-in. Not a failure. Just the subtle shift to the *we* language. No more othering himself.

Sam ached to push. To draw him into conversation about stepping out of the lab more than just here at the pole. Stop hiding. But he wanted Forrest to realize how good he was at it himself. See himself as a success rather than a failure.

"That's true. Even in the rural locations, you see at least a handful of chronic conditions, particularly with an older demographic." Sam looked around the quiet clinic. At any other place there'd be at least one person in the bay. It wasn't that there was an age limit on people employed at the pole, but most older people were either settled in their careers or with their family, or both.

"Speaking of places—" Forrest cleared his throat "—I can reach out to the lab and request a transfer."

"Transfer?" Sam blinked. Had he heard that right?

"Yes. The company has labs around the US and even in some foreign countries. There are no guarantees, but you're clearly not interested in Indianapolis."

"I never said that." Sam had made sure that he never said anything bad about Indiana. It was fine. And there were several trauma centers in the area.

Forrest raised a brow. "You've changed the topic every time I've brought it up over the last month. It's fine, Sam."

"Are you sure you want to go back to the lab?" Damn it. He hadn't meant to bring that up. Why didn't life have a rewind button?

"Go back to the lab? I am in the lab right now. Completing a study. I am not returning to bedside, Sam."

"But you're so good at it." Sam moved toward the desk.

Forrest pointed to an empty bay. "Yeah. Here, where it is normally quiet."

Sam flinched as the Q-word echoed in the empty area.

"With healthy patients." Forrest let out a sigh and leaned back in the chair. "As we just discussed, this is not a standard rotation. The burns Mark and Adina experienced were the exception, thank God. Hiding in the lab is good for me."

"I know you enjoy lab work, but…" Sam stopped not sure what else to say.

"But?" Forrest rolled his hand, his dark eyes blazing.

"I don't know. I just started but had nowhere to go. I just... I just..."

"Lost the words again?" Forrest pushed up off the chair. "I like the lab, Sam. It's my place."

"If it's so good, why do you keep using the word *hiding*?" Sam's brain slammed out the words.

Forrest paused, surprise evident on his face. "I say hiding because—" he hesitated "—I don't know. I just say it. I..."

"Hey!" The call came from the outer wall of the clinic. "Hey!"

"I shouldn't have said the Q-word." Forrest muttered the words behind Sam as they headed toward the call. A reprieve. But not the kind Sam wanted.

"She keeps vomiting. Can't keep anything down." Henry Polson, a researcher who spent most of his time out in the field was clutching a young woman who was having trouble holding up her head. "Kerry, keep your eyes open. Please."

Sam bent down to focus on Kerry while Forrest kept his attention on Henry. "Can you tell me when everything started?"

"Vomiting started twenty-four hours ago. We were out in the field, and scheduled to be there for the next two weeks."

Forrest knew that the field tents were technically climate controlled to withstand the harsh winter conditions of the poles. Understood that people needed to research the ice sheath. But spending weeks in the tents was where he wanted to be least in the world.

"Is anyone else sick?" Sam put his hand on Kerry's forehead. "No fever."

A good sign. This was probably a norovirus—it accounted for most stomach bugs. Unfortunately it was highly contagious. If Kerry was ill, others would start to show symptoms shortly. And out in the field was the worst place for them.

"No." Henry shook his head.

"Not yet." Sam looked at Forrest. The same thought clearly running through his mind.

Sam hooked a hand under Kerry's exhausted frame and guided her to a bed.

"Did the rest of the team come back from the field with you?" Forrest knew Henry wanted to care for his sick colleague, but they potentially had several other ill individuals ready to drop.

Most didn't need inpatient treatment with the virus. It typically cleared the system within seventy-two hours. But they were seventy-two hours of absolute hell. And Kerry would have become contagious the moment she showed symptoms.

The field had limited bathroom capabilities. It was roughing it in the coldest desert on earth.

Assuming she was the first, the others had one to three days before the incubation cycle completed itself.

"No. They're running experiments. We need—"

"You *need* to have them back here." Sam nodded to Kerry's feet.

Forrest took the sign and moved quickly to pull the heavy boots from her feet.

"Doc." Henry's strained voice echoed in the small bay.

"No." Sam shook his head, cutting off the argument Forrest saw brewing. "We'll get her stabilized, but you need to get them here. Now." Sam turned his full attention to Kerry.

"Henry..." Forrest motioned for the man to follow him out of the bay. "I know there are experiments to run." His words were soft, but the clinic was quiet and Forrest knew Sam heard him. His shoulders tightened briefly before releasing.

"If we aren't out there, the grant funding might get pulled. There are ramifications to delays." Henry pushed the hat off his head. "I know getting sick on the ice is unpleasant, but we have a real chance here to get core samples and make a difference. Understanding the shift in the ice sheath is vital to tracking the ocean's health. Losing a few days sets us back weeks. I know that sounds dramatic, but I'm telling the truth."

He didn't doubt that Henry was giving it to him straight. Forrest's experiments had a few days' incubation time to give samples time to grow, but there were still expectations of delivery that had to be met for his grants.

"I understand." Forrest rocked back on his feet. Given the conversation that had preceded this one, Sam was about to be pissed with him. "Is anyone else showing symptoms? Stomachache, vomiting, diarrhea, stomach cramps?"

"How are aches and cramps different?" Henry looked back over to where Kerry was losing the very little that was still in her stomach.

"Ache is constant. Cramps come and go. Are you asking because there are people experiencing either?"

"No. I just needed to know. Sound like the same thing."

Sam let out a noise but didn't call the man a liar.

Forrest didn't think Henry was lying. All doctors were scientists, but some were more focused on the science parts and others on the people side. It was a discipline that needed both.

"All right. How many are on your team now?" If there were too many, tracking this would be difficult.

"Six."

"Including you?"

"Yeah. Including me. It should be seven, but one guy always finds some reason to avoid field work—we made sure that our office back home is tracking that but there is nothing we can do here."

"Frustrating. But that means you're responsible for a manageable number of people." Forrest didn't react to the groan Sam let out. "You are to monitor everyone for the next seventy-two hours. Temperatures in the morning, at lunch, dinner and before bed. Everyone is to report to you if they have any of the symptoms I mentioned. If another member of the team reports the symptoms or has a fever over ninety-nine point seven degrees, you and the entire team are to report back to the station."

Henry looked at Sam then back at Forrest. "You sure?"

"Yes."

And no.

He was taking a risk. If there was norovirus running through the camp that was going to be very unpleasant. But no one came to the pole for fun. They were here for science. Important work that literally could not be done anywhere else.

And Sam is going to hate me.

He'd deal with that when this conversation was over. Add it to the list of things they needed to discuss.

"But I am serious, a single person reports a cramp and you pack it up." Forrest hoped his gaze carried how serious he was.

"Agreed." Henry swallowed then looked over Forrest's shoulder at Kerry. "You will take care of her?"

"Of course we will." Forrest patted Henry's shoulder. "Dr. Miller is the best in the business and our nurse practitioners are excellent."

"And you?" Henry's gaze caught Forrest.

His throat seized for a moment. "I'm capable of taking care of Kerry, too."

"Capable." Henry squinted at Forrest for a moment, then turned his attention to Sam. "Take care of her, Doc."

"Of course." Sam was already starting the IV with fluids and anti-nausea meds. "I'm setting a container right next to you—" Sam put her fingers on the metal bowl "—if you need it."

Kerry nodded but didn't open her eyes.

"We will be close by." Sam put the call button near her other hand. "But if you need something, press this."

Another nod from Kerry.

Forrest took a deep breath as Sam started toward him. But he didn't stop, just moved directly to the small desk the clinic maintained.

He followed, trying to let the annoyance flow out of him. "Sam."

"I don't want to hear it." Sam shook his head and started adding things to the tablet.

"There is a very good reason why I told Henry—"

"No." Sam's gaze burned as it met his. "No. There is not. You made a choice."

"I did." Forrest put his hands on the desk. "They have work that needs to be done."

"Yep. And six people with norovirus on the ice is a bad time, but the science *must* get done." Sam rolled his eyes.

"Hey." Those words felt like they were directed more at him than the team on the ice. "Sometimes it does have to get done. And we don't know that they have norovirus."

"Please. At least one of them does. The virus is contagious as hell and even a *capable* doctor is aware of that."

Forrest pursed his lips and tried to keep the angry words in check. "I am a capable doctor, but I prefer the lab. I am me, not some cookie-cutter piece than can fit into a carefully controlled perfect life."

Sam wanted him at bedside. And Forrest didn't understand why. He liked the lab. Was good at it. Better than he'd been at bedside.

"No life is perfect." Sam scoffed.

"Right." Forrest reached for Sam, but he pulled back. Forrest tried to keep the pain of watching that wrapped up tight. "And there is no way to control everything. If you can't accept—"

"Then you'll leave. Right? Just pack everything up and head to Indianapolis." Sam's words buzzed in the quiet.

"Sam."

"Forget it. Just forget I said anything. I need to take care of *my* patient." Sam grabbed the tablet and walked away.

Forrest didn't stop him. Didn't say anything as Sam walked past him.

What the hell?

CHAPTER SIXTEEN

FORREST HAD SLEPT in his own room last night. Not that Sam could blame him. He'd overreacted. But he hadn't been able to take hearing Forrest call himself "capable" while giving praise to every other member of the staff. It wasn't fair.

Forrest was wonderful. Gifted.

He was gifted before and ran when he thought he wasn't enough.

Sam sucked in air as he tried to force that brain worm out of his mind. It had wedged itself there. A reminder that Sam hadn't realized Forrest felt less than. He hadn't known that Forrest thought Sam deserved better. Forrest had just made the decision on his own and walked away.

Though if Sam thought about it, there had been signs last time. Not that their relationship was in trouble, but that Forrest was doubting himself. Little verbal cuts. Always directed at himself. Self-deprecating humor about how he wasn't enough.

Now he said he didn't know why he was using the word *hiding*. Did that mean there was part of him still unsure of his place like before?

Capable.

Was that another sign that he'd run one day?

Sam pushed his palms into his eyes, like the pressure could force the words out of his mind. The fears.

A knock on his bedroom door tore at him. It would be Forrest. Wanting to talk about yesterday. Iron things out. Sam pushed off the couch and walked to the door.

Time to fix what he'd broken yesterday.

"Forrest..." The man's name was out of his mouth before the door fully opened revealing Chris.

"Nope. Sorry. Is Forrest not with you?" Chris shrugged. "You two are always together. I just stopped by to ask if you were sure about releasing Kerry."

Sam was stunned by the question. He'd ordered her release for this morning, assuming she was hydrated. There was nothing they could do for her besides manage symptoms. And a hospital, even a tiny one, was full of germs.

She had a weakened immune system while the virus raged through her. It meant she was more prone to secondary infections.

"Is she not doing well?"

"She is." Chris let out a sigh. "Or as well as you can when you can barely hold anything down."

Sam shook his head. "So?" What was the issue?

"I don't know." Chris crossed his arms. "I just have this off feeling."

"Off?" Sam grabbed his coat and slid his feet into the boots he kept by the door. "What kind of off?"

"I can't explain it. I just... I don't know." Chris followed Sam down the hall and out into the cold toward the hospital. He did not elaborate on the way.

They walked in and Natasha stood, yawning. "I told him it was probably nothing."

"Nothing?" Sam took the tablet chart from Natasha. Kerry's temp was steady. She hadn't thrown up in more than six hours and had rested comfortably. She got dizzy when going to the bathroom. But that wasn't unexpected given the lack of sustenance in her body.

Everything looked like what he expected to see. "What am I missing?"

Natasha held up her hands. "Nothing." She pointed at Chris. "But he has a feeling."

Chris looked at the bay where Kerry was sleeping. "I don't know. I just…could it be something other than norovirus?"

"Like?" Natasha asked the question that was on the tip of Sam's tongue.

Chris looked at the bed and then back at them, "Ménière's disease? The chronic inner ear disorder. It can mimic a norovirus."

"Ménière's?" Sam looked at the chart. "There are only forty-five thousand cases of that disorder diagnosed a year worldwide. Has she complained of ear pressure or ringing?"

"No." Chris pushed a hand through his hair. "I know. I know."

"Chris, the most common answer is often the right one." Sam knew Chris was missing the pressure of a typical ER. Missing the pace and patient load.

The NP shuffled his feet and looked over at Kerry, still sleeping in the bed. "Yeah. Yeah. I told you it was nothing. I think I'm just bored." He zipped the coat he hadn't taken off back up and looked at the door. "My shift is over. You two enjoy." He waved and turned on his heel.

"You think he's okay?" Natasha didn't look at Sam as she asked the question. The closed door to the hospital was not going to provide any answers, but he understood her concern.

"I don't know. The ice affects everyone differently. He's working long shifts at night by himself, maybe we should switch it up, so that he isn't the only one pulling that overlapping shift."

"Oh, I am game to work more night hours." Natasha winked as she took the tablet chart from him. "I saw Kerry open her eyes. I'll start the discharge papers."

Sam let Natasha go as he ran through the symptoms of Ménière's in his mind. Kerry was presenting none of them except vomiting and dizziness. The dizziness was a direct result of the dehydration caused from the vomiting. Sam had no weird feeling. No concern about letting her go.

He let Natasha handle the discharge and got ready to spend the last part of his shift with Forrest. It would be fine. It would.

"Kerry gone?"

He hadn't said hello first when he stepped into the clinic. Sam shouldn't be surprised. Forrest was focusing on patients and that was the right move. But, somehow, after an evening of silence, he'd hoped for more.

"Yeah. We discharged her to her quarters this

morning. She's to rest and stay away from others for several days and to wash her hands thoroughly for the next two weeks. Hopefully that will keep the virus from running around the base." Sam pulled at the back of his neck as he ran out of things to discuss regarding Kerry. It would be nice if there were patients. Anything to cut the tension radiating between them.

"Have we heard from the field?" Forrest crossed his arms and then uncrossed them. At least Sam wasn't the only one who was feeling awkward.

"No. Maybe they got extra lucky." Sam shrugged. "More likely, they are ill but pushing through."

Forrest shook his head, "No, Henry would pull them back."

"You know him well?" He hated the bitterness in his tone. He'd wanted the whole crew back. Ordered it. And Forrest had figured something else out.

"No. But he cares about his team. It's why he brought Kerry himself. A leader who cares stays with their team in crisis, no delegation." Forrest seemed so sure.

"I don't know. We've both worked through illness." Sam wasn't sure why he was pushing this point. He should drop it.

But, if he dropped it, would Indiana come up again? Maybe. Maybe not. He wasn't sure which outcome he feared most.

"We are not the benchmarks for healthy work-life balance." Forrest blew out a breath, "Sam, about yesterday."

Sam waited for Forrest to say something. But no words came. Now it was Forrest lacking for words.

"Did you mean it when you said you'd put in for a transfer?"

Forrest pursed his lips. "I meant it yesterday."

Sam heard the hint of uncertainty and his stomach tightened. So he was already ready to run? "But today?"

Forrest looked at the hospital. "Not sure this is the best place for this conversation."

Sam's heart clenched. His soul fell apart. This was not happening again. Not again.

He shook his head. "I get it. We aren't soulmates."

"Excuse me?"

"Soulmates, Forrest. The other half of a person." Sam tried to focus on his breathing. Keeping air moving in and out of his lungs. Getting to the next second. And then the next.

"Soulmates aren't real, Sam. They're fiction."

"No. They are. My parents are soulmates and I thought…" Sam pinched his lips closed. "I didn't mean…"

"You did." Forrest took a deep breath. "Maybe you didn't mean to say it out loud. But you meant that you thought we were. But I don't fit in your life, do I?"

Sam shook his head, but it did nothing to quiet the buzzing in his ears. "What does that mean?"

"It means, you're trying to make me fit. Wanting me at bedside. Not talking about going back to where my work is. In the lab. You've always had an idea of what your life was supposed to look like."

"You're the one *hiding* there. How many times have you said that word since we landed on the ice? I wanted you to love your place. To realize how wonderful life is instead of wasting it. And I accepted long ago that my life wasn't going to look ideal." Sam had traveled everywhere to force the dream away. And all it had taken was Forrest landing on the ice for his heart to override his brain.

"No. You forced it to go dormant but never gave up on the idea of the perfect partner."

"Why is that so bad?" Sam blinked back the tears coating his eyes. Why was it so bad to want the person that fully completed you?

Forrest pursed his lips as he looked away. "Because I am not perfect. I'm broken and messy and unsure of so many things."

This was the moment. The place where he said he wasn't good enough. Where Forrest walked. Sam couldn't do it again.

"This isn't going to work." Sam rushed the words out. This time he was in charge. He wasn't getting left. He was choosing the path.

"Okay." Forrest nodded. "Okay." He looked around the empty bay. "I'm going to leave now. Call me if you get patients... Um, can I have the key to your room? I'll grab my stuff." He held out his hand.

Sam looked at it. He could walk this back. Fix it.
Soulmates wouldn't need fixing.

He dropped the key in Forrest's hand and closed his eyes so he didn't have to watch him leave.
Again.

* * *

"Soulmates. Soulmates." Forrest sniffed as he looked through the scope of the microscope. He'd known Sam for years and slipped back into the warm feeling of their life together so easily. But he'd never known the man actually *believed* in soulmates. That the word he'd always used to describe his parents had been completely serious.

It was a fanciful belief. A fairy tale. Relationships were work. There was no magical perfect person that made everything fall into place.

He'd worked with Natasha two days ago and Chris yesterday. He wasn't sure who'd be at the clinic when he arrived today. But he was certain that it wouldn't be Sam.

Two days of silence. Two days to revert back to the way they'd been the first month on the ice. He should feel something. Anger. Sadness. Relief.

But nothing came. No emotion. Just disbelief.

"You keep muttering and I'll have to call the clinic to report that you might be succumbing to ice madness." Charlee leaned against the wall.

"Ice madness is not a thing, Charlee." There was a phenomenon known as winter-over syndrome. The mental health diagnosis was not common, though not as rare as medical professionals would like, either. It came with hostility, insomnia and usually an absent stare that many called the long eye or Antarctic stare.

"I know. But you are muttering to yourself. Something about soulmates. You know, that annoying thing that Sam is for you even though the two of you are too stubborn to acknowledge it." Charlee rolled her eyes as she stepped closer to him.

That wasn't right. Couldn't be right.

"Soulmates aren't real. I wouldn't think that you would fall for such nonsense. A perfect person. Please." Forrest pulled up the screen of the electron microscope. He wasn't focusing through the lens, might as well shift machines and see if he could focus this way.

Charlee leaned against the counter opposite him. "Of course they're real."

Forrest scoffed. "You're a scientist. Please, you can't believe there is one perfect person for you. That if you can just find them, then everything is perfect."

"Two uses of the word *perfect*." Charlee looked at the image on the screen. "For someone who hates the word, and its implications, you're using it a lot this morning."

Was there a point to this conversation?

She held up a hand before Forrest could start his next argument. "I am a scientist. And no, I don't believe every soul is a puzzle piece looking for a match."

"Do you have a point?"

"Yes." Charlee crossed her arms. "You and Sam are still soulmates. Whether you or he wants to admit it. You balance each other. Or you would, if you could get over your personal issues."

Forrest huffed. "Sure. I can just magically morph into the perfect person. Throw all my flaws away and just be the right partner for Sam."

"And that right there is your problem." Charlee pushed off the counter. "Fix that and you might find life opens up a lot more."

"Fix what?"

But rather than answering him, she made a show of putting her headphones on and walking back to her station.

"Fix what?" Forrest raised his voice but Charlee didn't respond. "Fine."

He was supposed to be working. Not thinking of Sam.

Right, like I've ever gotten the man out of my dreams.

"Doctor Wilson?" Forrest turned, surprised to see Chris. Dark circles stood out under his eyes and he looked pale.

"Are you feeling all right? And why are you calling me Dr. Wilson?" He'd been Forrest to the team for weeks now.

"Part of Kerry's team came back last night. A supply run." Chris looked over his shoulder. "It's probably nothing but I have a bad feeling."

"Why? Were they sick?" If he'd misread Henry, Sam would be thrilled. No. That wasn't fair. He'd be upset that more people were sick on the ice. And he'd point out to Forrest that he'd screwed up.

Actually, he wouldn't do that, either. Forrest would know that all on his own.

"No. They're fine. Healthy." Chris rocked back on his heels. "I told Sam that I thought something else was up with her. I had no good reason. I still don't. But no one else on the ice is showing symptoms."

"All right." Forrest turned the microscope off. "Let's go check on her."

"Just like that?" Chris crossed his arms, then uncrossed them. "I might be completely missing this. I just—"

"Or you might not." Forrest grabbed his coat. He'd had worries that he hadn't followed through on before. The patient had always suffered. "Do you know her dorm room number?"

"Yeah." Chris led the way. His feet moving quickly for a man who'd clearly not slept because he was worried about a patient.

They reached her dorm room and Chris raised a fist and knocked. A solid knock. Then another.

"Give her a minute." Forrest put his hand on Chris's shoulder.

A minute went by and Chris raised his fist again. "We might need to get someone to open the door. If she's incapacitated." He knocked harder.

"Doctor Wilson? Chris?" Kerry called their names from the end of the hall. The wet hair meant she'd taken a shower and her coloring was far better than it had been. A patient on the mend. "What are you doing here?"

"Are you okay?" Chris looked her up and down.

"Yes. I mean the idea of food still makes my stomach turn a little. I think it will still be a day or two before I trust that what I eat will stay down. But overall…" She shrugged. "Are you okay?"

"Yeah." Chris nodded. "Sorry to bother you." He turned and started down the hallway. "I owe you an apology, Doc. I guess I let my mind run away with what-ifs."

Forrest understood. He'd been that doctor. The one who couldn't get past the what-ifs. The mess he'd made. "Which patient did you lose?"

Chris paused before heading to the door. "Patient? I've lost many. You don't work trauma without seeing it. Sucks, but no one is perfect. This one was just my imagination running away with me."

"Right." Forrest nodded. "I failed at bedside because I couldn't handle the what-ifs."

Chris shot him a look of confusion. "You work in a lab prepping the future of medicine. Your work may aid space travel in the future, but it will be invaluable to a lot of epidemiology studies. Hell, it might help prevent a pandemic. Hardly a failure, man. Sometimes, you realize you aren't cut out for certain kinds of work. Doesn't make it failure." He patted Forrest's shoulder. "I'm headed to my shift, but if what you do is failure, Doc, then what does that make the rest of us?"

He chuckled as he walked out. "Failure. Please."

Fix all my flaws.

Forrest's words to Charlee floated in his mind. This was what he was guilty of. He'd worked for years to see himself as enough. Gone through therapy, prided himself on believing he was open to the idea of marriage. Of spending his life with someone.

But Sam was right. He still joked about "hiding" in the lab.

Because part of me still feels like a failure.

Which was ridiculous. He loved the lab. Was so good at it. There was no need to denigrate the work he did. No need to put himself down.

But deep down, when Sam had gotten upset, he hadn't attempted to work it out. Hadn't waited to calm the conversation down. He'd let Sam walk away first. Asked for the keys to move himself out.

Believed he wasn't enough.

He'd walked away once. And Sam was looking for a reason he might walk away again. It was an easy pattern to see now. The hesitation on moving. The questions of Forrest's plans. And rather than reassure him, Forrest had walked. Just like Sam had feared.

Because deep down he worried he wasn't worthy of Sam. Wasn't enough for him, like he'd not been enough for his family. But Sam wasn't his family.

Forrest closed his eyes, if anyone walked by right now, they'd think he'd lost his mind just standing by a door doing nothing.

But his heart screamed as his brain listened, truly listened.

He and Sam belonged together. He looked at his watch, he had to finish the lab work but this evening they were having the conversation they should have had days ago. Years ago.

CHAPTER SEVENTEEN

"You were right." Chris walked into the clinic, his cheeks pink and eyes bright despite dark circles under his eyes.

"Right?" Sam didn't look up from the inventory he was taking. Again. He'd counted damn near everything in this place at least once. All to keep his mind away from the fact that Forrest had walked away from him.

Because I pushed him away.

"Yeah. Kerry had a norovirus. She is feeling a hell of a lot better." Chris waved to Natasha as she headed out the door. "See ya."

"She was in a hurry." Chris chuckled.

Probably sick of being around him. Sam was well aware that he was not good company at the moment.

"Her stomach issues were textbook, Chris." Sam put the swabs back in the drawer. There hadn't been a need for him to count each individual one, but it made the time pass.

"I know. I know. My feeling was ridiculous. But Dr. Wilson and I checked on her this morning. She looks tons better."

"It's been more than seventy-two hours. That's what should be happening." Chris had had a feeling, but Sam was positive that feeling was boredom.

In large trauma centers you typically saw two kinds of medical professionals. Those destined to burn out and move on and people that thrived on the stress. Adrenaline junkies, some might call them. Sam was never going to burn out at those facilities, but he didn't crave the never-ending patient load the way Chris clearly did.

Chris pulled up the tablet chart and let out an audible sigh at the lack of interesting news in it.

"Yeah. I know. But no one on the ice got sick and I just let my imagination run wild. I didn't want to bug you so I asked Forrest to check it out with me." Chris looked up from the chart. "Sorry, should I not speak about Dr. Wilson?"

Sam wanted to banish the man's name from the world. Or scream it into the void and beg the universe to reverse course. "It's fine."

It wasn't. Nothing felt like it was going to be right ever again.

"Well, you were right when you told me weeks ago that there is nothing wrong with realizing I wasn't cut out for certain kinds of work. I need the trauma unit. So that's where I will head back to."

Nothing wrong with choosing a new line of work. The words he'd said to Chris slapped him in the face. Had he been trying to force Forrest into the life he'd once planned? Two doctors working together. A partnership day and night. The life he'd given up.

Did I give up? Or did I start craving it as soon as we were back together?

"Am I a perfectionist?" Sam knew the answer as soon as he saw the look on Chris's face. "Don't answer that. I know the answer. Forrest accused me of trying to make him fit into my life. Of trying to force him out of the lab."

He snapped his mouth shut. He hadn't meant to say the last two sentences.

"Good grief." Chris shook his head before Sam could think of anything to say. "He mentioned failing at bedside this morning. Makes no sense. That man belongs in a lab."

So Forrest did still think of himself as a failure. Used the word *hiding* as a defense mechanism. A way to put himself down. And rather than soothe his worry, Sam had pressed him to return to something else.

"I mean you can be good at something and not want it." Chris clicked his tongue.

You could. Forrest was. Sam had been waiting for him to leave. Looking for signs. Forcing signs. So he didn't get hurt again.

I refused to talk about the future.

Refused to even plan a damn vacation. Of course Forrest would start to question his place in Sam's life. And as soon as Forrest had asked how he fit, asked about his place in Sam's world? Sam had run to avoid getting left again.

"Hey, I am…um…gonna go get a few hours of sleep. Call me if we get busy."

"We won't."

Sam lightly punched Chris's shoulder. "Probably not. But you're exhausted—don't tell me you aren't. And I've avoided working with Forrest for long enough. So I'll be back before his shift starts."

"Get some rest." Chris called as Sam headed for the door.

Sam planned to take a quick nap. As soon as he did two quick things. Two things he should have done days ago.

Forrest was going to see Sam as soon as his shift in the hospital was over. Natasha was working the night shift. Sam must have come on to the second shift since Chris had come to find him this morning.

He needed to finish this up and then find Sam. Hopefully, the shift would slip by quickly. If they weren't busy, it would at least let him plan out his apology speech. The one he'd mentally rehearsed for the last two hours still sounded cheesy.

"Doctor Wilson." Chris smiled as Forrest stepped in. "Good to see you." He turned to someone in the corner out of Forrest's eyes. "Your arrival means it is time for my nap. See ya!"

He winked at Forrest as he walked by.

"Natasha?" Forrest slid the shoes he kept at the clinic on. The quiet hospital sneakers that would weep if they saw the snow piles outside.

"No." Sam stepped around the corner.

He didn't look tired. Maybe he wasn't missing Forrest as much as Forrest was missing him.

Forrest's heart shut the worry down. He was not going to look for ways he wasn't good enough. Not with Sam. Not with anyone.

"The Virgin Islands." Sam grinned.

"Puerto Rico? Are we naming US territories?" Forrest raised a brow. What game was this?

"No." Sam stepped closer but didn't close the distance fully between them. "I want to go to the Virgin Islands for vacation before we head back to Indiana. Soak up all the sun on the beach. No winter coats! Though we should probably carve a weekend out for New York. My parents will never forgive us if we don't at least stop there."

Forrest closed the distance between them, put his hands on either side of Sam's face and brought him in for a kiss. There were still so many things to say. Apologies to be offered, but right now, here, in this moment, all he wanted was to kiss the man he planned to spend the rest of his life with.

"Wow."

Forrest would never mind Sam saying that after a kiss. "I'm sorry, Sam."

Sam put a finger over Forrest's lips. "I am the one that needs to apologize. I was stunned when you left. Hurt. And you were right—I had a plan for my life. I sought it out with Oliver and then pushed it aside for a while. But when you reentered my life—" Sam pressed his forehead to Forrest's "—it came roaring back. I don't think I even realized it, but I was so afraid you'd decided you weren't enough again."

"And I was so afraid that I had no place in your life that I walked away."

"I pushed you away. I was the one that said it wasn't going to work. I love you. All of you. And you belong in the lab, but I will forever say that you didn't fail at bedside. You aren't hiding. You just found your place. And that is beautiful."

Forrest sucked in a deep breath as those words knitted together a piece of himself. "I found my place. In the lab. But also—" Forrest knelt down "—at your side. I don't have a fancy ring. There is no place to buy one here. But I am never walking away from you, Sam Miller. Ever. Marry me."

Sam pulled him up, kissing him deeply. "Yes. Absolutely yes."

EPILOGUE

"Shake it!" Charlee walked up to Sam on the dance floor. "The tux looks great on you."

"Love looks great on him." Forrest wrapped his arms around him.

"I feel like you are a little biased, as my husband and all." Sam kissed Forrest as they continued to sway to the music with all their friends.

"Husband." Forrest lifted Sam's hand and spun him around. "I may never tire of hearing you call me that."

"I plan to hold you on that 'till death do us part.'" Sam pulled Forrest in as the DJ started a slow song.

Wrapping his arms around Sam's neck, Forrest kissed his cheek. "Easiest promise I've ever made."

"You two are sickeningly cute." Dr. Nicole Sapson spun by with her partner Shane Gibson.

"We're going to be just as cute next month." Shane kissed Nicole then winked at Sam and Forrest.

"Cuter. We better be cuter." Nicole laughed as Shane dipped her.

Forrest pulled Sam in for another kiss, "I don't think it's possible to be cuter than us."

Mark and Adina danced by them. The friends kept a platonic distance between them.

"Our wedding is a mini reunion." There was no place in the world Sam would rather be than here with Forrest, his parents and the friends they'd gathered at the pole.

"A South Pole Reunion." Forrest's lips brushed his. "Though the best South Pole reunion happened when we landed on the ice two years ago. I love you."

"That was as close to perfection as possible." Sam kissed his nose. "You're perfect."

Forrest dipped Sam as the music started fading away. "We're perfect. Together."

"Together."

* * * * *

*If you enjoyed this story,
check out these other great reads
from Juliette Hyland*

Falling for His Fake Date
Fake Dating the Vet
One-Night Baby with Her Best Friend
Dating His Irresistible Rival

All available now!